MAINA wa KĨNYATTĨ

DEDAN KĨMATHI SPEAKS

We will Fight to the Last Gun

DEDAN KĨMATHI SPEAKS

We will Fight to the Last Gun

Edited by Maina wa Kĩnyattĩ
Foreword by Ngũgĩ wa Thiong'o

Mau Mau Research Center
P.O. Box 746-00200
Nairobi, Kenya
Cell phone 0723-911-371
Email: info.mmrc@gmail.com

Copyright © Maina wa Kĩnyattĩ
First Published 1987
Reprinted 2009
Reprinted 2016
All rights reserved

ISBN 978-9966-1870-3-1

Cover design by Heavyconscious Movement

Distributed worldwide by African Books Collective

www.africanbookscollective.com

This book is available online under a differnt tittle:
Kenya's Freedom Struggle

Contents

Glossary of Gĩkũyũ Words 8
Abbreviations 10
Glossary of Historical Events and Persons 11
Foreword 15
Preface 21
Introduction 25

Part One

Fascism has Come to Kenya 45
We will Fight to the Last Man 47
This is the Voice of New Africa 48
Those Who Support the British Must Die 49

Part Two

Strategy for Armed Struggle 53
Proclamation of the KLFA's Political Position 54
Fraternal Solidarity and Support 57
Discipline and Unity 62
Combat Parochialism and Chauvinism 70

Part Three

There Will Be No Compromise 109
Letters to the Colonial Authorities 110
Letters to the Colonial Chiefs and Headmen 116
Letters to Tanganyika 120
Terms for Negotiation 123

Part Four

Firmly Demand the Total Withdrawal of British Forces from Our Country 133
Letters to the Kenya Parliament 134
Kīmathi to Guerrillas 139
Guerrillas to Kīmathi 155
Homage to Our Immortal Heroes 177

Part Five

Our History Should not be Distorted 181
Notes from Kīmathi's Diary 183

Part Six

We Were Betrayed 209
Time for Reflection 210
Epilogue 238

Dedicated To

All the Mau Mau Heroes and Heroines; they made the ultimate sacrifice on behalf of our people and our Country.

Glossary of Gĩkũyũ Words

Gĩkũyũ na Mũmbi	The original parents of the Gĩkũyũ people.
Gĩtungati	A guerrilla.
Gũkũ nĩ gwitũ	This is our country.
Gũtirĩ yuraga na ndĩkĩe	There is no rainfall that does not cease. Literally, every misfortune has an end.
Igongona	Agĩkũyũ customary ceremony.
Ĩrĩ kuuma kĩmamo ndĩcokaga	Once an animal has left its den, it cannot return. Literally means, once an animal is chased from its den, it does not return there.
Itungati	Guerrillas.
Kabaka	King of Baganda.
Kaburũ	A term of reference for imperialists, more specifically, Boers.
Kĩbandĩ/Kipande	Identity instruments, equivalent to the South African 'Pass'.
Kĩrĩnyaga	Mount Kenya
Matemo	Kĩmathi's undercover name.
Mbuci	Guerrilla camp.
Mĩrango ya Nderi	Nderi's gates.
Mũgumo	Tree considered sacred by the Agĩkũyũ.

Mūthiganwo nĩ ũrĩ nja Ndahonaga	This is a Gĩkũyũ proverb that simply means he who is sought by a man already in the courtyard has no way of escape.
Mwana wĩna mũreri ndarĩaga mai	A child with a guardian or parent does not live on shit.
Mwene-Nyaga	God
Ndagũthaitha na nguo cia nyũkwa	It is a Gĩkũyũ curse that, literally, means I beseech you by your mother's dress.
Ndongu	Wild fruits.
Ngai	God
Ngo	Shield
Ngongu to Karĩmatura	From Ngong Hills to Tula Hill.
Njohi	Gĩkũyũ Beer.
No kinya tũmonorie	We will kill them. This means that we will pour their lives down.
Panga	This is a Kiswahili word for a heavy machete used as a weapon or cutting tool in East Africa.
Thai Thathaiya Ngai Thai	Peace with God.
Thayũ wa Ngai	Peace of God.
Thũmbĩ	A Gĩkũyũ traditional hat.
Tigwo na wega	Goodbye

Abbreviations

EAS	The East African Standard
INA	Ituma Ndemi Army
KAR	King's African Rifle
KAU	Kenya African Union
KCAE	Knight Commander of African Empire
KCGE	Knight Commander of Gĩkũyũ Empire
KDC	Kenya Defense Council
KLFA	Kenya Land and Freedom Army
KP	Kenya Parliament
KPGC	Kenya Parliament Guard Commandant
MKP	Member of the Kenya Parliament
MM	Mau Mau
MMCC	Mau Mau Central Committee
NNR	New National Regulations
PWD	Public Works Department
SWC	Supreme War Council
WC	War Council

Glossary of Historical Events and Persons

W.W.W. Awori: Editor of a Kiswahili language newspaper, *Habari za Dunia,* he was the vice-president of KAU from 1952 to 1956, and the member for Nyanza in the colonial Legislative Council. He compromised and cooperated with the colonial regime during the war of independence.

Bamũinge: Mau Mau General who refused to abandon the struggle after independence; he was killed in an engagement with the Kenyatta neocolonial regime.

Baraza: The oldest Kiswahili weekly in Kenya, it ceased publication in 1979. The newspaper was founded by the colonial government in 1930 to serve as a propaganda instrument to mobilize African support for imperialist occupation as well as a tool to sabotage the anti-imperialist struggle.

Baring, Evelyn: Colonial governor of Kenya, and commander-in-chief of the imperialist forces at the beginning of the Mau Mau liberation struggle.

Beecher Report: Intended to serve as the blueprint for African education in colonial Kenya; this racist report was vigorously opposed by nationalist forces and the people of Kenya in general. It meant to kill initiative and vitality of Kenyan youth making them hate their culture and heritage, turning them into buffoons with petrified minds.

Brockway, Fenner: Labour Party politician and anti-colonial activist.

Carothers-Henderson theory: D.C. Carothers was a colonial government psychologist who wrote a notorious and racist pamphlet, *The Psychology of Mau Mau,* which argued that the Mau Mau liberation movement represented a return to a barbaric narcissism among the Agĩkũyũ. Thus the Mau Mau oath was conveniently portrayed as a symptom of psychological deviation, Gĩkũyũ mental disease. A similar theory is to be found in Ian Henderson's *The Hunt for Dedan Kĩmathi* and L.S.B. Leakey's writing.

Cege Kîbacia: A Veteran Kenyan Trade Unionist. He was also the founder and president of the African Workers' Federation until he was deported to Baringo from 1947 to 1957 for union activities.

Colonial Orders: A reference to the colonial villages which were set up in Central Kenya to isolate the KLFA guerrillas from their supporters among the peasantry.

Gakure wa Karûri: A major collaborator with the colonial authorities in Mûrang'a District. In other words, he was a puppy of the colonial regime.

General G. Erskine: Commander-in-Chief of the British colonial forces in Kenya during the war of national independence.

Kenyatta's theory of forgive and forget: After independence, Kenyatta embarked on what he called a programme of reconciliation; his philosophy is summed up by the title of one of his books, *Suffering Without Bitterness*.

Khama and Mutesa: Sir Seretse Khama was exiled from the then Bechuanaland by the British colonial authorities in 1948, and he was not allowed to return until he renounced his chieftaincy in 1956. Similarly, the Kabaka of Buganda, Sir Edward Mutesa, was exiled from Uganda in 1953 for refusing to cooperate with the British imperialist occupiers on a new constitution.

Land Consolidation Act: Land Consolidation Act (popularly known as the Lyttleton Plan). Date of assent was July 17, 1959. It was a colonial law, officially intended to amalgamate land holdings in Central Kenya in order to weaken the MM movement, and at same time to promote the interests of national traitors—the law was seen by supporters of the Mau Mau as just another calculated attempt to take away more African land.

Levellation: The term was derived from the English word, 'level'. As Karari Njama informs us, "Homeguards and other traitors were regarded as stumps in a field, to be leveled or gotten rid of". See Barnet and Njama (1966: 77).

Glossary of Historical Events and Persons

Longonot Mountain: A volcanic mountain (about 10,000 feet high) situated in the Kenya Rift Valley, 45 miles from the great city of Nairobi.

Loyalists: This term was used to refer to the Africans who supported the British imperialist occupiers, in general, but more particularly to the homeguard traitors.

Lyttleton plan: See Special Commission to Kenya, below.

Makhan Singh: Famous Kenyan Trade Unionist of Indian descent.; he came into prominence in 1937 when he organized a two-month strike in Nairobi as the secretary of the Labour Trade Union of East Africa.

Mathenge: He was appointed by the Mau Mau Central Committee to be the commander-in-chief of the Kenya Land and Freedom Army when the war for independence started in 1952. His military HQ was in Nyandarwa forest. In August of 1953, he was demoted and Kĩmathi took the KLFA overall commander. In 1955 Mathenge was killed by the British force in Nyandarwa.

Mau Mau and civilization: See the Carothers-Henderson theory, above.

Mbiyũ wa Koinange: KAU leader and its official representative in the UK from 1951 to 1959.

Moscow Society: It was a counter-revolutionary group organized by the colonial state to sabotage the Mau Mau movement from within. In order to sabotage the movement, the Moscow Society sought to liquidate the main leaders and cadres of the movement, in order to weaken it internally and aggressively by trying to link the Mau Mau with the Soviet Union Communist Party, and to justify to the capitalist world that the Mau Mau, who were fighting for their country that was stolen from them in front of the entire, and had nothing to do with communism, was a communist movement.

Mũhoya wa Kagumba: Chief Mũhoya was Dedan Kĩmathi's godfather. When the Mau Mau war of national independence started, Mũhoya joined the British forces against the national anti-imperialist movement. The

British armed him and made him a colonial chief; he was a killer of the people.

Mount Kenya Front: Known as the MEI Mathathi Army, this KLFA front was made up of guerrillas from the Mathĩra region, Nyĩrĩ, Kĩrĩnyaga District and from Embu Mũrũ and Ikamba. These forces were under the command of General China.

Reforms: Allusion to the Lyttleton plan, see above.

Reserves: With the expropriation of the so-called white highlands, it was colonial policy to restrict Africans to specially-designated areas called 'reserves', in which they would provide a pool of cheap labour.

Special commission to Kenya: This resulted in the Lyttleton plan of 1954, which proposed a multiracial council of ministers with one African member.

Wameru: The Wameru, who are of Tanzanian nationality, live around Kilimanjaro; they are not to be confused with the Merũ of Kenya.

Wat Tyler Rebellion: The peasant revolt in England in 1381 bore many similarities to the liberation struggle in colonial Kenya. Both were directly ignited by the desire for land among the peasantry, and, more indirectly in the case of the Kenyan liberation struggle, hash taxation.

The Yatta Plateau: The Yatta Plateau is located on the dry plains in Eastern Kenya, which became a place for resettlement and exile for those who had been uprooted from their homes by the British imperialist occupiers. Located in the Tsavo National Park, the Yatta Plateau has the world's longest lava flow that runs along the western boundary of the park.

Foreword

Why is history subversive?

Human beings make history by their actions on nature and on themselves. History is therefore about human struggle: first with nature as the material source of the wealth they create—food, clothing and shelter; and secondly, struggle with other humans over the control of the wealth. Labor, human labor, is the key link between the two struggles. It is labor, with all the instruments and accumulated skills that makes wealth out of nature. The struggle among humans is over control of the entire organization of the production, exchange and distribution of the fruits of labor.

Development in society is brought about by changes in the human struggle with nature; and in the social struggle. The changing social formations, institutions, values, outlook, reflect the ever-changing relationships between labor and nature, and between social groups in one nation and between nations.

Change, movement, is hence the eternal theme in history. It is the universal expressed in all the particularities of the various nations and people of the earth over the centuries. Therefore, no society is ever immobile: there is movement all the time since the two relations or struggles are constantly in motion. History, therefore, is constantly reminding The Present of any society that all things, good or bad, shall come to pass. Tomorrow will be The Present; and The Present will be The Yesterday.

But it is precisely because history is the result of a struggle and tells of change that it's perceived as a threat by all the ruling strata, in all the oppressive exploitative systems. Tyrants and their tyrannical systems are terrified at the sound of the wheels of history. History is subversive. And it is because it is actually subversive of the existing tyrannical system that there have been attempts to arrest it. But how can one arrest the wheels of history? So they try to *rewrite* history, make up *official history;* if they can put cottonwool in their ears and in those of a population, then maybe *they,* and *the people,* will not hear the *real* call of history; nor will they hear the *real* lessons of history, so as not to repeat the errors of yesteryear. Kenya, under British colonialism, and now under neocolonialism, is a good example of what happens when a population deflects the historical truths of yesteryear in order to pacify a system of exploitation in the present that is doomed to repeat the errors of the past.

If there is one consistent theme in the history of Kenya over the last four hundred years or so (that is since the sixteenth century), it is surely one of the Kenyan peoples' struggle against foreign domination. At various times and places, they have fought against the Arab, Portuguese, and British invaders. The British invasion in the 19th century and their colonial occupation in the first half of the 20th Century were accompanied by the heroic resistance of Kenyan people of all nationalities. Some names, like those of Waiyaki wa Hinga, Koitalel Arap Samoei, Muhammed Abdille Hassan, and Mekatilili wa Menza have become legends. Brilliant battles were fought during these invasions and occupations. The fort, built by Bukusu nationality around Mount Elgon, known as Getambe, for instance, still stands today as a reminder of Kenya's heroic tradition of resistance and struggle.

During the years of British settler occupation, the resistance continued, acquiring a new character because a new class, a wage-earning class (a proletariat) was born with colonial capitalism. The new working class joined hands with peasants and tried to forge links with the workers and peasants of all the nationalities to overcome the divide-and-rule tactics of British colonialism. The highest peak of this heroic tradition of resistance was the armed struggle initiated and carried out by the Kenya Land and Freedom Army (KLFA), otherwise widely known as Mau Mau. The supreme leader of the KLFA was Dedan Kîmathi.

But, of course, there has been another tradition SELL-OUT, traitorous tradition whose highest expression was in the actions of the homeguard, loyalist collaborators with the British enemy, which are continued in the neocolonial system suffocating millions of Kenyans today.

British colonialism tried to cover the true history of Kenya. They tried to rewrite Kenya's History to justify their invasion and subsequent occupation of the country. The Kenya Land and Freedom Army, was the first of its kind in the post second world war period in Africa; the KLFA became the focus of British propaganda, to prevent an armed struggle from becoming a model as a form of resistance. The British even trained some Kenyans and brought them up to look at Kenyan history with the eyes of the British bourgeoisie. The British propaganda history consisted of burying the real tradition of struggle and, erecting in its place, the tradition of loyalist collaboration. Loyalist historians were praised, and even honored, while the people's historians were incarcerated.

The attempt to bury the living soul of Kenya's history of struggle and resistance, and the attempt to normalize the tradition of loyalism to imperialism has continued into neocolonial Kenya. The loyalist colonial homeguard of yesterday are the neocolonial Mbwa Kalis (guard dogs) of imperialism today. There have been two types of history in Kenya: the *Real Living* History of the masses and the approved official history of those who do not want the truth told. Those who run neocolonialism (those who today have even given military facilities to the leader of world imperialism, i.e. the USA) are mortally afraid of any symbols or reminders of the Kenyan people's history of struggle and resistance. And naturally, KLFA (Mau Mau) and Dedan Kîmathi, as the highest symbols of that tradition, have received total official neglect or distortion.

The two types of histories have produced two types of historians. These are the official historians, the approved historians, whose role is to give national legitimacy to the tradition of loyalism and collaboration with imperialism. These have received accolades and honors.

But the Kenyan people's real history of struggle and resistance has also thrown up its historians. First are the ordinary people who, in their songs, poems, sayings, anecdotes, remembrance, still talk of the Waiyakis, the Koitalels, the Me Katililis, the Hassans and the Kîmathis of Kenyan history; and secondly, a few progressive intellectuals who have negated their roots among the petty-bourgeoisie, and joined the people. These have put their learning, their intellect, at the service of the people. They are committed to unearthing the buried history of struggle and resistance.

In Guyana we have the example of Walter Rodney; but in Kenya we have the example of Maina wa Kînyattî. Since his return to Kenya in the 1970s, Maina wa Kînyattî saw his role of being the ears and eyes of the people, as far as this concerned their history, their truth. Whereas the official state historians borrowed eyes and ears from the colonial and neocolonial heritage, Maina wa Kînyattî and other patriotic historians, borrowed their ears and eyes from the people. Maina wa Kînyattî travelled extensively in Kenya. He spent many an evening and weekend in the homes of those who had fought the British, and who were now condemned to living in hovels, and on the edge of starvation. He recorded their stories, verbatim; and they in turn trusted him as a real living historian that would report the truth. They started giving him documents they had hidden for years, documents many had long forgotten. They gave him information they had kept among themselves for fear of an official, neocolonial, wrath. They knew that those holding the reins of power in post-independent Kenya were those actually sabotaging the struggle for independence, and they were leery about whom they should divulge any information to, for fear of the unknown. But here was a historian who seemed not afraid; who was talking their language of a struggle that was not being documented correctly.

The papers Maina wa Kînyattî was able to rescue are contained in this book. They speak for themselves. They need no introduction, or defense of explanation. It s a record of how the participants, the Kenya Land and Freedom Army, saw the struggle as contained in some of their written documents.

Theirs was a national struggle – for land, independence, freedom from hunger, freedom from foreign control; freedom from external and internal social oppression – and they put their lives at the service of those ideas of political liberation.

They were completely surrounded by the enemy. Unlike the armed liberation movements that followed them in Africa (in Algeria, Mozambique, Angola, Guinea-Bissau, Zimbabwe, etc.) they had no rear bases or supply bases in neighbouring countries, for the simple reason that these were also under the same colonial enemy. Their bases were entirely among the Kenyan people.

For arms they depended almost totally on what they could capture from the British army, and on their own factories in the liberated and semi-liberated zones around Nyandarwa and Kĩrĩnyaga.

Again, the KLFA barely had access to national and international propaganda to counter the stream of lies coming from the British settler colonial regime in Kenya and the Colonial Office in London. In the country, the KLFA depended mostly on word of mouth to explain their case and the progress of the struggle to the Kenyan people. But still, with all the limitations under which they operated, they tried to keep written records of these activities; and to establish written communications with the national and the international community was not always an option afforded to the KLFA.

Some of the documents were later captured by the colonial enemy. Some were destroyed, or distorted. Some are still held in secret by the British government, and the neocolonial regime in Kenya. But some escaped capture; and it is to the credit of Maina wa Kĩnyattĩ that he has managed to recover a number of these letters and documents and put them at the disposal of Kenyan and international community.

When the history of the armed liberation struggles in Africa is finally written, KLFA will stand supreme, not so much because of the heights it reached, or the depths from which it rescued Kenya and Africa from, but because of its will to take back what belonged to the Kenyan people, its land. KLFA (Mau Mau) was the first organized armed blow against imperialism in Africa. It paved the way for the many African countries that fell victim to European colonialization, with such brilliant results in Algeria, Mozambique, Angola, Guinea-Bissau, Zimbabwe, and South Africa.

Maina wa Kînyattî has now paid a price for his work in Kenya history in 1982, he was arrested, and imprisoned, for six years. He just about escaped the fate of another historian of the people, Walter Rodney from Guyana. But has he? He is losing his eyesight, thanks to years of incarceration without the right to sun light. His health has been deteriorating, in part to the horrid conditions of prison in Kenya; conditions in Kenya prisons are among the worst in the world.

Those who had imprisoned him were hoping that he would lose sight of the Real history of Kenya. But they were wrong. These documents and his other works like *Thunder from the Mountains, Mau Mau Patriotic Songs* and *Mau Mau: The Peak of African Political Organization in Colonial Kenya* will always stand as a memorial of his commitment and courage to the struggles of Kenya.

But even if they were to silence Maina wa Kînyattî, would they silence the history of Kenya? Would they arrest, imprison the living history of Kenya? This history is being written by the millions of workers and peasants of all nationalities in Kenya, who in their actions and songs are saying NO to imperialism and its comprador alliance in Kenya. The spirit of the Kenya Land and Freedom Army and its leader Dedan Kîmathi is being reborn in Kenya today!

History IS subversive because TRUTH is! The unavenged father's ghost of Kîmathi's struggle and his KLFA walks the days and nights of today's neocolonial Kenya. The masses know it. So, do the ruling comprador bourgeoisie; hence the continuing repression, and its opposite—RESISTANCE. The 1980s and 1990s will see the conflict played out to its logical conclusion—liberation from neocolonialism. These papers will play their part in that struggle by providing lessons from the weaknesses and strengths; the failures and the successes of the past.

Ngũgĩ wa Thiong'o
Stockholm, 1986.

Preface

It was Dedan Kĩmathi's strong belief and wish that the political and military work of the Mau Mau movement should be documented and preserved for posterity. Connected with that, Kĩmathi insisted that the KLFA front commander should send a written monthly report on his unit's activities, including the minutes of all meetings held in his *mbuci* (camp), to the Kenya Parliament. Similar instructions were given to all Mau Mau leaders in the villages and urban centers. In keeping with this policy, Kĩmathi appointed field secretaries to tour all guerrilla camps and battlefields and to document the activities of the guerrilla army.

From the time he was made KLFA Field Marshal, Kĩmathi made it a habit of writing down his daily observations of the independence struggle in a personal diary; he also filed all the communications he received and copies of letters and documents he wrote. At the same time, he made sure that the minutes of every session and General Conference of the Kenya Parliament (KP) and the Kenya Land and Freedom Army, the military wing of the Mau Mau movement, were set down. 'These documents', he once told the KP members, 'will be concrete evidence that we fought and died for this land'.

To preserve these historical materials, the KP established underground archives in Nyandarwa forest in 1953, and appointed guerrilla experts to man them. General Omera was appointed the director of the archives department. Thus, the first truly national archives in Kenya was established.

However, a most unfortunate incident occurred early in 1955; Gen. Omera was captured by the enemy in the battlefield, and after being viciously tortured he surrendered. He led the British forces to the underground site of the archives in Nyandarwa, and entire collection of Mau Mau records was captured. According to the enemy's newspaper, Baraza, of August 27, 1955:

> Mapema mwaka huu jeshi la Serkali lilishambulia maficho katika msitu wa [Nyandarwa] yaliyotumiwa na Dedan Kîmathi. Kati ya vitu vingi vilivyopatikanako kulikwa na makaratasi mengi na vitabu vingi kama vinavyoandikwa katika skuli vilivyokuwa vimetumiwa na Kîmathi kwa kuandika matokio.
>
> Mahali pa maficho ya Dedan Kîmathi palijulikana kwa majeshi ya ulinzi kama matokeo ya habari zilizotolewa kwao mwaka 1954. Baada ya kujulikana mahali penyewe, yalionyeshwa hasa picha ya kupigwa kutoka eroplenini na halafu walikwenda huko.
>
> Early this year, government forces attacked a camp used by Dedan Kîmathi in the [Nyandarwa] mountains. Among the numerous things found in the camp were papers and exercise books used by Kîmathi to record events.
>
> The location of Dedan Kîmathi's camp was discovered by the armed forces as a result of information received in 1954. After the location was known, the camp itself was pinpointed through pictures taken from an aeroplane; then government troops moved in.

The captured documents and letters, written in Gîkûyû, Kiswahili and English, were intact and well-preserved in four sacks. With the help of their African running dogs, the British colonial authorities translated and indexed the documents, and then collated them into 14 volumes of about 30 pages each. They were filed under the title: 'The Dedan Kîmathi Papers'. Copies of these documents were sent to the British M.I.5 and the Public Records Office in London, and a copy was deported in the Kenya colonial archives in Nairobi. None of these documents have been made public to this day.

Obviously, the British occupiers had concrete reasons for not wanting to avail these revolutionary documents and letters to the public. First, they confirm, in no uncertain terms, the heroism of the Mau Mau movement and its armed wing, and the tremendous support that Kîmathi had among

Preface

the Kenyan masses; they also expose the brutality of the British imperialist forces and some of the many defeats they suffered at the hands of the Kenya Land and Freedom Army. Secondly, these texts describe the British imperialists and their Kenyan collaborators (to borrow Fidel Castro's words), "in terms which they deserve and with words that cannot be erased from history". What is more interesting, however, is the fact that the government of independent Kenya has collaborated with the British imperialists in their efforts to conceal this glorious chapter of Kenya's history. These texts, and many others dealing with Mau Mau, are "classified materials" in our own 'national' archives; and under a joint British-Kenya agreement, they were 'supposed' to be made public in 2013, but this is 2016 and they have yet to be made public.

Is the whole affair then a cover-up, a conspiracy to protect those Kenyans and British settlers who committed murder and other serious crimes and atrocities against the Kenyan people during the war of national independence? Indeed, it is a mystery that the rulers of an independent country should have agreed to withhold such important information from the Kenyan public. It is also shocking to know that large quantities of Mau Mau documents and historical photos were destroyed shortly after independence.

In an attempt to unearth this mystery, I was able to obtain some original texts and copies of these documents from some Kenyans who had them in their private libraries. I also managed to photostat quite a few of the Mau Mau documents held in libraries and academic institutions abroad. A few of the documents and letters included here have also appeared before, in contextually distorted form, in some bourgeois newspapers, periodicals and books.

Because I was not able to obtain the whole collection of the Kĩmathi papers, some of the documents and letters included in this volume remain incomplete, these texts are factually accurate and wholly authentic. I have refrained from altering them in any substantial way. My role as a translator and editor has been simply in make them consistent and legible.

These texts were written by, and were for, those thousands of unnamed Kenyans who joined forces in the patriotic war against British colonial occupation. Their study will, therefore, make us more aware of the development of the armed struggle in Kenya, its political weakness and strength; Dedan Kîmathi's relationship with his guerrilla comrades, workers and peasants; his political understanding of the social forces around him; and his undying love for his homeland. From these texts, we will become aware of the great sacrifice Kîmathi and his comrades-in-arms made for the liberation of our country.

In summary, the main purpose of publishing these documents is twofold: first, I believe it is a matter of simple academic responsibility for me to make available to the Kenyan people documents and letters of such national and historical importance in the hope that this new information will help to stimulate serious research on the subject among Kenyan intellectuals. Secondly, I want to preempt the publications of a distorted, pro-colonial version of "The Kimathi Papers", which might be aimed at reinforcing the Carothers-Henderson anti-Mau Mau theory. In the process, I want to undermine the anti-Mau Mau arguments that are being propounded by a handful of pro-imperialist Kenyan intellectuals in our national universities.

Introduction

The dialectic of colonial repression has proved that... no colonialist aggressor can overcome peoples who are determined to win their freedom.

Amilcar Cabral

To wage a revolution is to annihilate what is bad, and build what is good...Our revolutionary work is, therefore, not yet completed, because these evils still undermine and sabotage the constructive process of the revolution.

Ho Chi Minh, 1952.

After the formation of the Kenya African Union (KAU) in 1944, the nationalist movement began a concerted, largely legalistic, struggle for changes in the system of government in the country. Toward this goal, the KAU leadership effectively mobilized a considerable segment and strata of the Kenyan masses as the first step in the acquisition of political and economic power. Their ultimate political aim was a government of the majority; they sought political dialogue with the British imperialist regime in pursuance of this fundamental aim. Although the nationalist goal of the KAU leadership mainly reflected petty-bourgeois outlook, the party was able to heighten the national, anti-imperialist, consciousness of the majority of the Kenyan masses through numerous political activities and mass campaigns. But its immediate political objective was never the overthrow of British colonialism through armed struggle. The majority of the KAU leaders, including Jomo Kenyatta, did not understand that imperialism is a violent monster, which has to be fought violently; and were hence determined to use constitutional methods in their efforts to achieve majority rule.

This approach to Kenya's anti-imperialist struggle was fiercely opposed by a number of KAU militants—men like Bildad Kaggia, Fred Kubai, J.D. Kali, James Beauttah, Stanley Mathenge and Dedan Kîmathi and the anti-imperialist leaders of the working class movement, particularly Cege wa Kîbacia and Makhan Singh. The only road to national independence, for these patriots, was through armed struggle. Their stance reinforced Kim II Sung's thesis: "History has not yet seen any instance of imperialism making a gift of independence to colonial peoples, nor any case of a people deprived of their country that received independence from others without waging armed struggle".

The divisions and contradictions within the national anti-colonial movement brought about the birth of the Mau Mau underground movement in the 1950s. In other words, the Mau Mau movement was secretly organized by the KAU militants, as an outright rejection of the Kenya African Union's non-violent methods of struggle. Kaggia tells us why: "... Mau Mau (MM) was an organization formed by KAU militants who had lost faith in constitutional methods of fighting for independence... It was clear [to us] that the [British] Government would never give up Kenya without an [armed] struggle".

The movement was initially organized from Nairobi, which were the headquarters of the Central Committee (CC) and the main base of its revolutionary activities. When the Mau Mau Central committee (MMCC) was set up in 1951, it was composed of twelve members, with Eliud Mūtonyi as the chairman, and Isaac Gathanju as the secretary.

The CC was the supreme organ of the revolutionary movement and was responsible for its overall policies. Through the Group of Thirty (national congress), county and village committees, the CC mobilized, and gave political education, to hundreds of Kenyans, especially workers and peasants in central Kenya (the old central Kenya), Narok District and the European occupied region of the Rift Valley province. In the process, it exposed the contradictions between the interests of the Kenyan people and those of the British imperialist occupiers.

The military wing of the MM movement, which was later named the Kenya Land and Freedom Army (KLFA), was under the command of General Stanley Mathenge; his deputy was General Enoch Mwangi. It was a small force of about 300 fighters based in Nairobi. During the early period of the movement, the primary duties of the KLFA were: **1)** to help the CC in mobilizing the masses against British occupation; **2)** to recruit Kenyan youths into the MM underground, particularly the KLFA forces; **3)** to eliminate the enemies of the movement; **4)** to collect funds, weapons and strategic information for the movement; and **5)** to give military training and political education to MM cadres.

From the beginning, MM leaders used oathing as a major political weapon in politicizing, educating and mobilizing the Kenyan masses against the British occupiers. The oath served not only as a political instrument, but also as a tool to strengthen and enforce discipline and maintain security in the armed movement. Thus, the first oath (the Oath of Unity) bound the recruits in the following words:

> I will never reveal the secrets of this organization, or anything concerning this organization, to the colonial authorities or to any persons who is not himself a member; and if I violate this vow, may this oath kill me.
>
> I will obey without question all the rules and regulations of this organization, and should I ever transgress against them, may I die.

Aside from its function as an effective tool in ensuring obedience, loyalty and truthfulness to the Mau Mau leadership, the MM oath was also a pledge to uphold national patriotism:

> I swear in the name of our country, in the name of this movement, that I will use all my power for the total liberation of Kenya from British imperialism, sacrificing my own and my family's lives. I shall never reveal the names of members of this movement nor those of the leaders, even if I am caught, tortured or killed. I shall always be loyal to the leaders of the movement. If I betray this vow, I shall deserve every punishment meted out to me as a traitor.

Such an oath, administered in the name of the country and people of Kenya, was an expression of the true patriotism and an uncompromising commitment to the national liberation. To make sure that the oath was effective, the punishment for those who broke it was taken seriously by the leadership. For the first offence, a man or woman would be warned. Second offenders would be liquidated. It was felt that only through the threat of this severe punishment could the CC leadership be assured that its rules and regulations would be obeyed (Mathu, 1974: 21).

As a patriotic, revolutionary movement, MM subjected its cadres to rigorous discipline, self-sacrifice and self-denial. Every cadre was required to participate fully in all the movement's activities, obey all rules and regulations without question, and carry out its decisions without compromise. Thus, ran one of the movement's pledges:

> Should I ever be called, at any time, to go and kill the enemy of this movement, I will arm myself and proceed to fulfill the orders thus given to me by the leaders. I shall never compromise the principles of this movement.

In terms of financial support, every MM member was required to surrender all his wealth to the movement without hesitation:

> I swear before God and the compatriots present here today, that all my wealth – land, livestock, money, etc – belongs, from now on, to the movement. I will offer all my strength and energy in order to further the cause of the movement. If I violate this vow, may I be killed.

After the British declared war on the Mau Mau on October 20, 1952, and arrested some of its Central Committee members and all key KAU leaders, including Kenyatta, the movement went further underground, and its leadership was reorganized and strengthened. The CC was transformed into a war Council (Kenya War Council), and its headquarters were moved from Kiburi House to Mathare Valley, then a major base of the Kenyan working class. Under its new organization, the duties and responsibilities of the War Council were to coordinate the movement's war effort, mainly to provide the guerrilla army with men, weaponry, medical supplies, clothing and strategic information; and organize more underground cells in the urban centers and the rural areas. The War Council was also charged with reinforcing discipline in the movement, and with the elimination of all its enemies, traitors, spies and informers; the recruitment of more members, and the organization of an elaborate system of agents, whose task was to infiltrate the colonial machinery in order to obtain firearms and strategic information, was also an essential responsibility of the War Council.

Within the War Council a new body, the Legal Committee, consisting of three leaders and three military commanders, was formed to deal with legal matters within the movement. At the same time, the 'Group of Thirty' was enlarged and reconstructed into a powerful committee known as the Central Province Committee (CPC), under the direction of Gĩcohi wa Gĩthua. Basically, the CPC was to function as the national congress of the movement. All the districts in central Kenya and the city of Nairobi were represented in this committee, but it also had members from the European occupied area of the Rift Valley province, Ukambani and Narok. The CPC's main task was to assist the War Council in coordinating the revolutionary process.

The KLFA forces, under General Mathenge's command, entered the Nyandarwa forest in June 1953 to begin a national war against British occupation, and in December 1952, Dedan Kĩmathi, at the age of 32, joined Mathenge's forces in Nyandarwa. Another KLFA front was opened in Kĩrĩnyaga forest under the Command of General China.

In the early period of the war, Kĩmathi helped General Mathenge in organizing and strengthening the guerrilla army in Nyandarwa. Under their supervision, many guerrilla camps were established, including the Kariaini *mbuci*, which had more than 3,500 guerrillas, and was to become the headquarters of the Kenya Land and Freedom Army under Mathenge's leadership.

Kīmathi drafted the rules and regulations governing these camps. Because of his literary skills, it was his responsibility to maintain contacts with the the War Council in Nairobi on matters dealing with new recruits, firearms, clothing and medical supplies. It was also his responsibility to contact the Mau Mau village leaders, whose duty was to supply food and strategic information to the guerrilla army. The nature of Kīmathi's work meant that he was always on the move—visiting guerrilla camps, talking to the peasants, and organizing attacks against the foreign enemy.

Two weeks after the Battle of Naivasha, which took place on March 20, 1953, a three day conference was held at the Gīthugī camp in Nyandarwa to discuss the war efforts in detail, and to celebrate the Naivasha victory. The conference was attended by 250 guerrillas, including Kīmathi and Mathenge.

Kīmathi, who opened the conference, called upon the guerrillas and the people of Kenya to fight with unceasing determination in order to expel the British imperialist occupiers from the country; other speakers included Mbaria wa Kaniū, China and Mathenge. This was the first major conference held by the guerrillas since the inception of the armed resistance. In the ensuing discussions, the KLFA leaders agreed that in order to strengthen the armed struggle, the recruitment drive would have to be intensified, and more fronts had to be established in the country. Furthermore, it was decided that all the existing guerrilla units would immediately be brought under General Mathenge's command. A resolution was also passed establishing a twelve member Supreme War Council (SWC), with General Mathenge as Chairman and Commander-in-Chief of the KLFA forces; Mbaria was appointed as General Mathenge's Deputy; Kīmathi the SWC Secretary-General and Mūraya wa Mbuthia as the Deputy Secretary.

It was clearly established at the conference that the SWC would function temporarily as a High Command of the armed movement until a general conference was held to form a more permanent war council. Kīmathi was appointed the convener of the first KLFA congress. At the end of the Gīthugī conference, SWC members were instructed to tour all the guerrilla camps and explain the proceedings of the conference; each SWC member was assigned to cover a specific region. Kîmathi was assigned three districts—Mũrang'a, Kĩambu and Narok. Accompanied by Mbaria, he visited all the existing guerrilla camps in Mũrang'a, where he met district's KLFA Front Commanders, principally Generals Matenjagwo, Kago and Ihuura. But his journey to Kĩambu and Narok was cancelled because of a lack of enough contacts.

On August 16, 1953, in accordance with the decision reached at Gĩthugĩ, Dedan Kîmathi called a four day congress: letters concerning the meeting were sent to all guerrilla commanders. However, according to Karari Njama, when Mathenge received his letter, he was furious at Kîmathi for calling such an important gathering without first consulting him. Mathenge argued that since Kîmathi was his 'clerk', he had neither the power, nor the right, to call any guerrilla meeting without his authority. He accused Kîmathi of plotting to take over the leadership of the KLFA armed forces. Consequently, Mathenge decided to boycott the congress and tried to use his position to sabotage it, but without success.

Mathenge's line on this issue was incorrect. From all indications, Kîmathi was not motivated by personal interests; his exclusive commitment was to the liberation of our homeland and, in this connection, he was thoroughly aware that the only way to drive out the British occupiers from the country was through the unity of all Kenyans, and particularly the unity of the guerrilla fighters. His ardent patriotism is evident in a conversation he had with Karari Njama soon after being informed about Mathenge's decision to boycott the congress. He told Karari:

> Mathenge has lost a great chance to be known to many guerrillas…I hope he is not suffering from megalomania. I would certainly attend any meeting he would call me to. I would like to meet him and resolve our differences…Nevertheless; I will postpone nothing due to his absence (Barnett & Njama, 1966:235).

Later, he told the members of the Kenya Parliament that:

> Although I have never mentioned his name in this Parliament before, there is nothing wrong with Mathenge. I would not like to cause any ill-feelings because he might think I consider myself superior to him. I always like speaking well of people because I am not perfect. He is still doing his work, and he is a brave and active leader. Those helping me [to lead the struggle] are all efficient leaders and we have one target. But I want to make my position very clear. My concern and responsibility is for the people of Kenya, for those comrades who have decided to sacrifice their lives for our land and freedom. I have no other ambitions.

The congress was held at Mwathe in Nyandarwa, and was attended by more than 5,000 guerrillas and a large number of local peasants. In the course of the discussions, the delegates support the formation of the Kenya Defense Council (KDC) to replace the SWC. Dedan Kîmathi, a charismatic and resourceful leader, was elected the council's President and Field Marshal of the KLFA forces with Macaria wa Kîmemia, as the Vice-President; and Kahiu-Itina, as the Treasurer and Gathitū wa Waithaka, as the Secretary-General. In total the KDC Executive Committee was composed of twelve members. Mathenge and Mbaria were dropped from the leadership altogether.

Essentially, the KDC was designed to function as the vanguard of the armed movement, and was charged with the following duties: **1)** to deal with the overall planning and coordination of the military campaigns; **2)** to be responsible for the overall discipline and political direction of the revolutionary movement; **3)** to strengthen and maintain contacts and communication with the War Council in Nairobi, which was mainly responsible for recruitment and the financing of the armed struggle; **4)** to work closely with Mau Mau village leaders, who were supplying the guerrilla army with food, strategic information and mass base; **5)** to function as a propaganda machine for the liberation struggle; **6)** to keep a record of all the movement's activities for future generations; and **7)** to be in charge of the promotion and demotion of fighters.

On the second day of the congress, the delegates' major task was to identify the armed forces of the movement. Eight armies and their areas of operation were identified. They were:

Gĩkũyũ Iregi Army (GIA), Mũrang'a
Ituma Ndemi Army (INA), Nyĩrĩ
Kenya Inooro Army (KIA), Kĩambu and Narok
MEI Mathathi Army (MMA), Kĩrĩnyaga forces
Kenya Levellation Army (KLA), a KLFA unit based in the Nyĩrĩ countryside under Commander Kariba
Mbũrũ Ngebo Army (MNA), the Rift Valley Army
The Townwatch Battalions (TW), all the urban KLFA forces
Gĩkũyũ and Mũmbi Trinity Army (GMTA), small KLFA units operating in villages and towns of central Kenya

Broadly, the KLFA was divided into three armed wings: the forest guerrilla wing, based in the Nyandarwa and Kĩrĩnyaga forests; the urban guerrilla wing, with its headquarters in Nairobi; and the peasant detachments based in the rural area of central Kenya and the European occupied region of the Rift Valley province.

The backbone of the movement was largely made up of peasants, workers and unemployed youth, who dauntlessly supplied it with new recruits, shelter, weaponry, medicine and important intelligence. In organizational terms, the MM movement derived much of its strength, energy and courage from tightly-knit and well-disciplined cadres in the towns and countryside.

As we have mentioned above, the Kenya Defense Council was the KLFA High command in the forest and was under Kĩmathi's leadership. The Nairobi KLFA forces were under the leadership of General Enoch Mwangi. These forces were divided into small columns; they were hence able to carry out swift attacks against the foreign enemy and national traitors, and then disappear among the people for safety. It was the revolutionary duty of the Nairobi KLFA forces to conduct vigorous campaign against the forces of exploitation and oppression among the working class; they were charged with the task of distributing propaganda leaflets; of giving military training and political education to new MM cadres before they joined the main guerrilla army; of enforcing discipline in the movement; and of guaranteeing the security of the members of the War Council.

Because of vicious attacks on the liberation movement and the arrest and detention of Key Mau Mau leaders in Nairobi, the KLFA headquarters were moved to Nyandarwa in January of 1954 under Kîmathi's leadership. At the same time, the Kenya Parliament, which was formed in February of 1954 to replace the Kenya Defense Council, became the supreme organ of entire armed movement.

With an elaborate and formidable network of field secretaries and couriers who kept him in contact with the KLFA leadership in Nairobi, the frontline commanders, the village detachments and the Kenya Parliament, Kîmathi began the armed struggle against a technologically advanced British army. Kîmathi had apparently learned the lesson which Fidel Castro was later to articulate:

> The only way a small, poor country can defeat a large, technologically advanced country is to mobilize, educate, and organize the whole population to resist.

As the KLFA Supreme Commander, it was his duty to write to frontline commanders, KLFA village unit commanders, and the War Council in Nairobi, to explain developments in the struggle. For instance, after the surrender of General China to the British forces on January 15, 1954, Kîmathi sent a circular to all KLFA commanders explaining the position of the Kenya Parliament vis-à-vis that of General China and the colonial authorities. To justify his surrender to the enemy, General China had written a two page-letter to Kîmathi asking him to call off the fighting and to cooperate with the British imperialism. In reply to General China's letter, Kîmathi said:

> My soldiers will never leave these forests until the British government accepts our demands to:

1. Disarm its forces unconditionally.
2. Release all the political prisoners.
3. Recognize our country's independence.

Similarly, writing to General Kago, Kĩmathi told him:

> Did you receive the circular I sent to all frontline commanders concerning General China's surrender? China has agreed to collaborate with our enemy, to work against the homeland, to save his neck. In order to prove his loyalty to his new friends, he has written to all Mount Kenya Frontline commanders and the member of Kenya Parliament urging them to call off the fighting and surrender to the British forces. I received a copy of his letter and when I read it, I was filled with indignation. If China thinks that I will mortgage this great struggle to save his life, he must be crazy.

However, most of the letters Kĩmathi wrote were strategically aimed at strengthening the armed resistance and politicizing guerrilla fighters. Thus, he sent the following lines to a guerrilla comrade: "...you should be proud of your black skin because the keys of a piano always give the sweetest music..." Again: "...you have done well to understand that our country and the people are the dearest things in the world. I advise you to support, with dedication, the great struggle of our people. It will lead us to self-government and the recovery of our stolen land. Do not follow those who preach peace and submission. Follow the truth; as you know, a man dies but truth lives forever..."

Some of Kĩmathi's letters deal with the strategy of the liberation struggle: how to obtain ammunition and guns from the British forces, how to ferry medicine, clothing and food to the guerrilla army in the forest, and how organize workers, peasants and unemployed youth around the national liberation struggle. To quote one of the letters he sent to Colonel Wamũgũnda:

Try to put every effort into organizing food for guerrillas. We need plenty of ammunition because I don't want to see the guerrillas walking around with empty rifles. The cadre who goes to Nyũrũ town for ammunition should go regularly...Tell the women to make us sweaters, for the place is very cold; ask them to supply us with the following items: sugar, coffee, salt, tea-leaves, matches, soap and above all, medicine...The medicine you sent me is finished and my teeth are still aching. Please send me some more.

In the section of the text dealing with strategy, I have also included the letters sent to Field Marshal Dedan Kîmathi by his comrades-in-arms. Most of these letters dealt with the nature of the national, anti-imperialist struggle, discipline among the fighters and cadres and the contradictions between the enemy and the masses of Kenya. Broadly speaking, these revolutionary letters constitute the most important chapter in Mau Mau history. For the first time, we are able to understand the dialectical relationship which existed between Kîmathi and his men. It is clear from these documents that Kîmathi was a popular leader, and that the guerrillas viewed and recognized him as their undisputable commander and teacher. In this respect, any guerrilla who had problems or needed some advice could write to Kîmathi for assistance. Let us quote one of the letters sent to Kîmathi by a guerrilla in need of help:

> Dear D.K.,
> I have no blanket. The one I had was taken away by Juma; he said he would give it to Karari to bring it back to me, but I've heard that Karari has gone to Rũthaithi for a mission. I've only a raincoat, but it is not enough because this place is very cold. If you have one extra blanket, please send it immediately. I will be waiting for it.

Major Kahiga wrote the following lines to Kîmathi:

> Dear Marshal,
> Your only fault is that you send your Generals maize and wheat

flour, but never remember to send them cigarettes. If you have some in the store, please send them to me. Things are not bad; we are doing our revolutionary work as usual. When we are not fighting, we concentrate mostly on making guns...

Kĩmathi received many letters of this type, but he also received reports like this one:

> To D. Kĩmathi,
> Wamaitha joined my battalion in August of 1953. I have given her permission to go home to Gĩthi, Nyĩrĩ, on November 1, 1954, because she is pregnant. I have asked colonel Wanjohi to escort her to her village. She was living with comrade Rũkũ as his wife. Due to her efficiency and patriotic commitment, I have promoted her to the rank of captain.

In part, Kĩmathi's responded:

> ...It is against KP's regulations for the commander of the unit to give his men new ranks. That is the task of the Kenya Parliament and me.

Possibly the most revolutionary letters Kĩmathi received were from Colonel Wamũgũnda. In reading these Colonel's letters, no one doubts his revolutionary zeal, commitment and patriotism. It is also worth observing that Colonel Wamũgũnda was very much aware of the importance of discipline and secrecy in the revolutionary process. Writing to Kĩmathi, he said:

> ...There is something important I would like to share with you. I hope you won't mind. As a Supreme Commander of the KLFA armed forces and the leader of the national movement, you should be very careful and disciplined in what you do. Every step you take should be well-calculated. You should always suspect those you meet, even your own relatives...In short, what I am trying to say is that discipline and secrecy are our greatest weapon in this unequal war.

Kĩmathi's response to Colonel Wamũgũnda:

> ...I take your advice seriously. I will do my best to tighten my loose discipline and to follow, to the letter, KP's rules and regulations...As I told you the last time we met, even if we go trouserless, eat grass and tree barks, we will uphold national patriotism and continue fighting until we drive the British occupiers out of our beloved country. But if we all die before achieving our fundamental goal—our country, our rivers, our mountains, and these valleys and forests, shall testify for our heroism and undying love for our homeland.

Revolutionary songs and poems were also composed in the forest and distributed amongst the guerrillas and their supporters in the country. Here is one of the poems:

> I try to forget and to wipe
> The memories out of my mind.
> I die every moment.
> I see her picture.
> I tried to persuade her
> To join me in the forest,
> But she refused.
> Now she is no more.
> The homeguards tortured her,
> They killed her.
> Will I ever find peace
> Of mind without her?
> She was mine,
> But she was unkind.
> She was so unkind,
> Although she was mine.

Kĩmathi wrote the following lines, entitled: "We Fight To The Last Gun" and circulated among the KLFA frontline commanders:

We are a patriotic army.
We are a people's army.
We shall never kneel.
We shall never bow.
We shall never bend.
We shall never compromise.
We shall never give up
a piece of our national soil.
We shall fight to the last gun.

Between 1953 and June of 1956, the British authorities wrote several letters to Kîmathi calling for peace negotiations. In reply, Kîmathi consistently demanded that before any peace conference could take place, the British would have to withdraw their forces from the country and disarm their Kenyan allies. In a letter to the District Commissioner, Nyĩrĩ, Kîmathi said: 'To make my position clear, peace can be restored in this lovely nation only if your government withdraws its armed forces from our country unconditionally."

Similarly, he wrote to colonial chiefs like Makimũ (Kĩambu), Njiiri (Mũrang'a), Eliud Mũgo (Nyĩrĩ), Ndũng'ũ Kagori (Mũrang'a), Mũhoya (Nyĩrĩ), Ignatius Mũraĩ (Mũrang'a), and other high-ranking colonial agents, warning them that they would pay with their lives for their treacherous support of British colonialism. He urged them to stop killing their people, and to unite with them in fighting for the liberation of the country. In a letter sent to one colonial headman in Nyĩrĩ, he said:

I really pity all of you who are collaborating with the British— the enemy of our country. Being surrounded by trenches, daily parades and subjugated to rigid order, you suffer more than those of us who are championing the people's cause. But why suffer for crumbs? How terrible it is to die as a traitor!

Meanwhile, the spread of Mau Mau into Northern Tanganyika (now Tanzania) forced the colonial government there to declare a state of emergency in the region, and to order the mass deportation of Gĩkũyũ,

Embu, Mĩĩrũ and Kamba workers to Kenya. Under these circumstances, some of these Kenyan workers suspected of being Mau Mau members were mercilessly tortured, while others were murdered. Many were sent to the Manyani detention center.

In his effort to counteract the British anti-Mau Mau propaganda in Tanganyika, Kĩmathi wrote to certain African political leaders and some colonial chiefs there, asking them to reject imperialist propaganda and to support MM struggle. In a letter to Salehe Kibwana, he stated:

> It is not true that we are against civilization, that our aims are to take our people back to ancient times. Our fighting is for the return of our stolen land and freedom. If you remember, the Europeans have occupied our best land and reduced us to slavery...We are not savages or murderers as the British continue to claim. We know what we are doing and we know what is best for our people.

Kĩmathi also wrote to liberal individuals in Kenya and the rest of Africa urging them to support the Kenyan anti-imperialist struggle. He contacted the governments of Egypt, India, United States, France and the former Soviet Union, and progressive individuals abroad, in an attempt to build international support for the liberation movement. Some of these communications are included in this collection.

Thus, Kĩmathi's major task from the moment he assumed the KLFA leadership was to speak for the national liberation movement, to articulate its aims and goals. In this connection, he published several articles in newspapers such as the *East African Standard*, *Citizen*, *Habari za Dunia* and *Rhodesia and East Africa*; he also authored a series of pamphlets and circulars which were widely distributed in the country, particularly in central Kenya, Nairobi city and the European occupied area of the Rift Valley. The two documents: 'The New National Regulations' (NNR) and the 'KLFA Charter', which are included in this collection, were among the major documents Kĩmathi wrote and circulated. Both texts were issues in late 1953.

The NNR document was meant to rally the Kenyan masses around the liberation movement. Whilst it strongly urged the African masses—workers and peasants—to revolt against British colonial occupation, it also called for cooperation and unity among the African people, regardless of their social positions. It made it very clear that any Kenyan who sided with the British occupiers would pay with his or her life.

The KLFA Charter, on the other hand, was a national political manifesto for the liberation movement, and was hence widely circulated in the country and throughout the world. The document was specifically sent to the British authorities in London, to the governments of India, Egypt, France, the former Soviet Union and the United States. George Padmore of the Pan-African Congress in London; W.E.B. Du Bois, Chairman of the Pan-African Congress in the United States; Kwame Nkrumah of Ghana; Fenner Brockway, the liberal British Member of Parliament; and Mbiyũ wa Koinange and Joseph Murumbi, the KAU representatives in London, each received a copy. Kĩmathi requested Mbiyũ and Murumbi to present the KLFA charter to the United Nations on behalf of the people of Kenya. We have no evidence that this was done.

Despite its nationalist world outlook and its lack of a theoretical and ideological analysis of world imperialism and capitalism, the KLFA Charter took a very strong anti-imperialist line. Apart from outlining the position of the national liberation struggle, the document made it very clear that the people of Kenya would continue fighting until they drove the British imperialists out of the country. The document concluded with the following remarks on the Wat Tyler Rebellion in Britain:

> Do you not remember what your grandfathers did during the reign of King Richard II, when sixty thousand slaves [serfs] went to [the King] and demanded their freedom? These people tore down prison walls and the houses of the rich men they hated, and killed many who were their enemies. They burned the houses of the lawyers, tax collectors and King's Officers who had wronged them, and killed many men of that sort, cut off their heads, put

them on poles and set them up on London Bridge. [Because of their resistance] the King made them free forever...

Internally, the KLFA leadership worked tirelessly to consolidate the national resistance. For instance, circulars and directives concerning discipline among the guerrilla fighters were sent to all KLFA frontline commanders. At the same time, the KLFA field secretaries were dispatched to the battlefield to record the activities of the guerrilla army. In addition, a series of meetings and consultative conferences were held in the Nyandarwa forests to discuss the war efforts and to draw up new strategies and tactics. The minutes and reports of these historic meetings and conferences clearly show how the national liberation struggle was structured and organized, especially the important role played by the Kenya Parliament in the development of the guerrilla army.

Kenneth Watene's play, *Dedan Kimathi*, and Barnet & Njama's book, *Mau Mau From Within*, like Ian Henderson's book, *The Hunt for Kimathi*, portray Field Marshal Kîmathi as a lone, sadistic, dictator, who used his position in the movement to eliminate those comrades who criticized his leadership, but the study of the KLFA minutes and reports in this collection will vividly show that the KLFA leadership was very democratic, and well structured, and that like any other KLFA leader, Kîmathi was criticized when he took an incorrect line. Equally so, as the 'Notes From his Diary' show, Kîmathi was very much concerned with the financial state of the movement. He tried to keep a record of every cent spent on the struggle; he was not a rogue or a thug as the enemy of our homeland portrays him. He led the movement with characteristic, revolutionary vigor, commitment, dedication and patriotism.

Ideologically, the Mau Mau movement, as Kîmathi's writings show, was based on patriotic nationalism rather than on the theory of dialectical materialism. During the early stage of a national, anti-imperialist struggle, nationalism is a positive element--it is a force to rally the oppressed masses around the national liberation movement. However, it eventually poses the danger of channeling the people's struggle away from class struggle and socialism because of its ideological limitations. For instance, because of its nationalist world outlook, there was no ideological struggle within the MM movement to transform nationalist consciousness into class consciousness, nor was there a serious and systematic analysis of imperialism, the class struggle, and the relation of socialism to the Kenyan revolutionary process. As a result, the MM revolution was halted by the comprador bourgeoisie in league with world imperialism before the working class consolidated its proletarian base.

Algeria, like Kenya, provides a good example of this failure: since the armed resistance against French imperialism was based on nationalism, it was easily hijacked by the bourgeois nationalists and the revolutionary process was quickly halted before the masses acquired real power. As Amilcar Cabral, who was himself a guerrilla leader, observed:

> The ideological deficiency, not to say the total lack of ideology, within the national liberation movements – which is basically due to ignorance of the historical reality which these movements claim to transform – constitutes one of the greatest weakness of our struggle against imperialism, if not the greatest weakness of all.

Clearly, there is nowhere in the world where a nationalist ideology has succeeded in consolidating the power of the working class by overthrowing the forces of imperialism and capitalism; and successfully establishing a socialist government.

Kĩmathi and Kĩmathism

Kimathism represents what it means to be a Kenyan — reaching for new heights and reaching for what is Kenyan. It heightens our people's patriotism and anti-imperialist consciousness and deepens their love for the homeland.

PART ONE
Fascism has Come to Kenya

We will Fight to the Last Man

Editor's note: On October 21, 1952, after the British occupiers declared war on the people of Kenya, the Mau Mau Central Committee secretly distributed a leaflet in Nairobi entitled, *We Will Fight To The Last Man*, which resounded like a battle cry; it states:

Fellow compatriots: Since 1920 we have tried to regain our freedom peacefully, but all of our efforts have come to naught. The British are not interested in constitutional negotiations. Now, they have arrested and imprisoned our leaders, proscribed our political party and declared war on us.

We will fight them, compatriots. Let those who have guns use them. Let those who have spears use them. Let those who have swords use them and let those who have *panga, rungu* and arrows use them. Cowards should be eliminated.

It is better to die fighting than to compromise our struggle for independence. Our basic aims are:

1. to overthrow colonialism and foreign domination;
2. to win national independence and form our own government;
3. to abolish forced labor, colonial taxes and racial oppression; and
4. to create a new society based on democracy.

Compatriots arise!
Resist foreign occupiers.

This is the Voice of New Africa

Editor's note: On October 23, 1952 the Mau Mau Central committee secretly issued and distributed the following leaflet in Nairobi City and other major towns in the country. It was addressed to the 'Murdering Colonialists' and was entitled, *"This is the Voice of New Africa"*. It reads:

You must feel very happy at the outward success of your cruel operation. You arrested our leaders and a lot of other people. Thousands of Africans leading a normal life have been stopped, searched, beaten, humiliated and arrested. Creating the Emergency, you have brutally treated us and now you cannot claim democracy and freedom. Fascism has come to Kenya.

We have been robbed of all freedom. You have destroyed our press by arresting our editors and suppressing our newspapers. The brutality and oppression, the show of force and the rule by the gun, will not stop us from our goal. You cannot end our political wish by arresting our leaders. We have many more men with brains and will continue to fight you and achieve our freedom. This is the voice of new Africa.

We have been forced to go underground. If we are known, you will murder us. We are not afraid. We ask how many of us will you imprison, and how many of us will you kill? We are six million and power is in our numbers. We shall retaliate in the method you have employed. We shall not forget the bad treatment we are suffering. When our time comes we shall not show mercy because you do not know what mercy is. We will kill you like you are murdering us today. This is not threat; it is a fact, because it is how we are feeling today.

Africa unite!
Signed: Kenya War Council

Note: Officially, the colonial General Attorney, John Whyatt, denounced the revolutionary leaflet as the "work of terrorists" and made it clear that any newspaper reprinting it would be prosecuted and any individual found in possession of the document would be arrested and imprisoned (Maina wa Kĩnyattĩ, 2010: 134).

Those Who Support the British Must Die

Editor's note: On March 21, 1953, the KLFA force attacked the enemy camp in the Lari village, Kīambu County, and with little resistance the guerrilla army captured the camp. The enemy defenders, seventy of them, including their commander Chief Luka surrendered and were immediately put to death; the guerrilla army lost none. The following morning, British and native loyalist forces entered the village and massacred hundreds of civilians, including women and children, and then blamed the Mau Mau for their well-calculated, savagely, atrocities. Before the guerrillas withdrew they set the camp on fire and distributed a leaflet in the village explaining the reasons for their mission and action. It was entitled, *Those Who Support the British Must Die*. The following is an extract:

We have taken an oath that those who hinder us from our revolutionary activities and help the whites must die as they sleep together with their wives and children, and their property destroyed as if a great rainstorm had come and their footprints have been washed out forever and ever. If any person disobeys what is decided by the movement and continues to assist the British [occupiers], we must castrate him, take his eyes out, cut his head off, and see if his British master can bring him back to life. Luka's elimination is another warning to those others who stand in opposition to the motherland. We will not hesitate to wipe them out ruthlessly.

We shall never lay our arms down until our country is free and independent.

This is where we stand.

Signed: Kenya War Council
H.Q: Nairobi
March 21, 1953

MAU MAU INTELLIGENCE SERVICE AND COMMUNICATION SYSTEM, 1954-1957

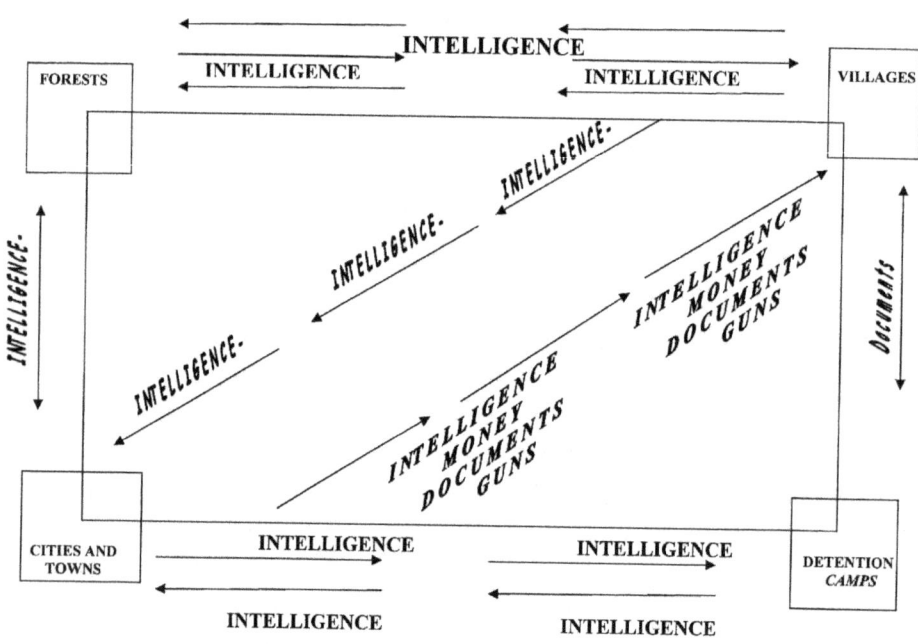

MAU MAU INTELLIGENCE SERVICE AND COMMUNICATION SYSTEM, 1951-1953

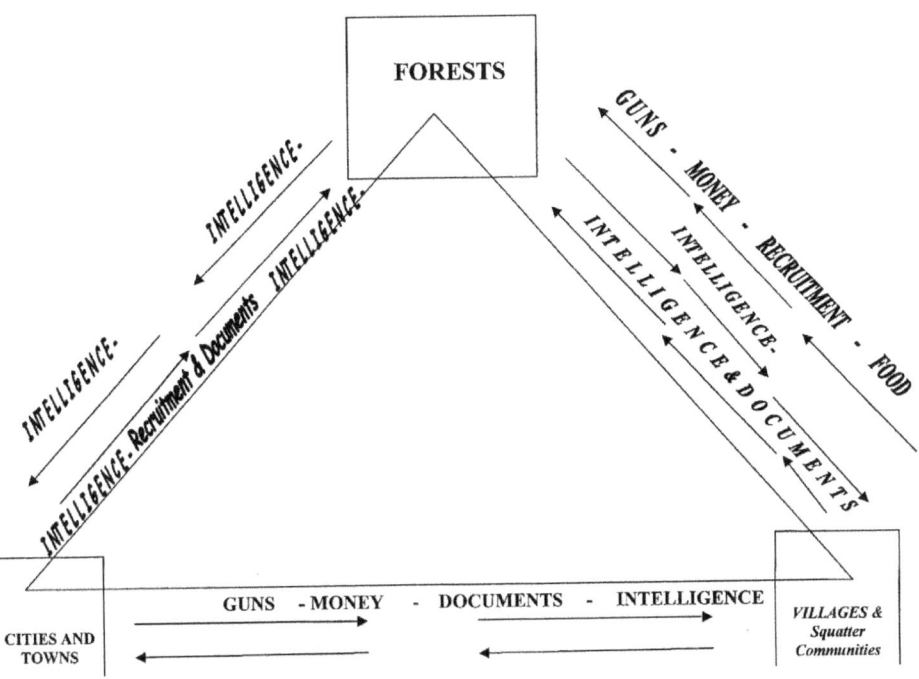

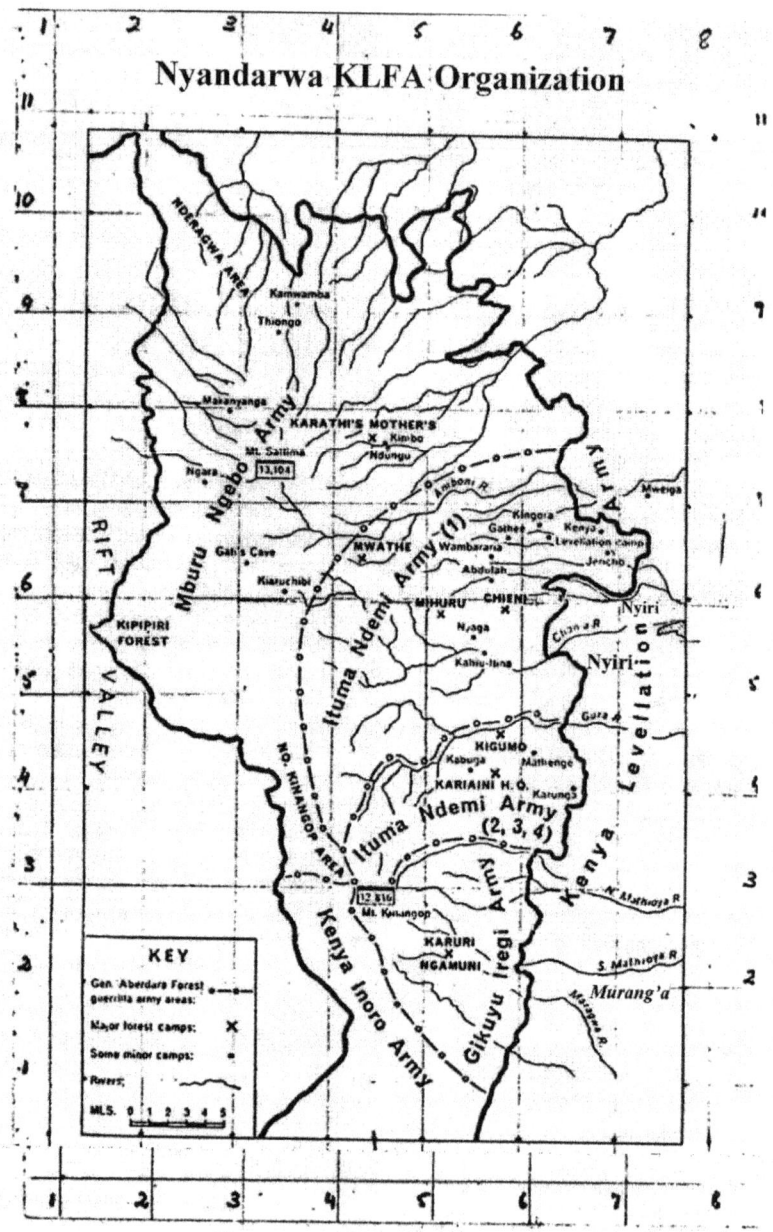

Courtesy of Barnett & Njama

PART TWO
Strategy for Armed Struggle

Proclamation of the KLFA's Political Position

New National Regulations

The Europeans who govern Kenya have killed many Africans and stolen their cattle, sheep, goats and land. They have enacted anti-African laws, and they have justified the burning down of many African homes; they have illegally removed many of our compatriots from their land. These sinister acts have caused great suffering and many deaths amongst our people—suffering which we shall never forget or forgive.

In order to fight this brutal enemy successfully, the Kenya Defense Council calls for cooperation and unity among the African population. The KDC also urges the African people to stop killing one another, to stop supporting the colonial occupiers. If any African, be he a policeman, a KAR soldier, a homeguard, a chief or an ordinary civilian, disregards this call, he will be severely punished.

Below are the new regulations:

1. No African shall pay taxes to the white man and his government;
2. No African shall be employed by the White man in towns and/or in the rural areas;
3. No Africans shall obey the laws of White man, or seek protection from his government;
4. No African shall join the homeguard, KAR and police forces, unless he is working as under-cover for the MM underground;
5. No African is allowed to trade with the White man or establish any economic cooperation with him; and
6. Taxation Act: From January 1954 onwards, Africans shall start paying taxes for the development of their country to the Kenya Defense

Council. Only women and children are exempted. This act also applies to all Europeans, Asians and Arabs who reside in the country. The tax payments will be as follows:

i) Africans, 15 shillings per year

ii) Asians and Arabs, 30 shillings per year

iii) Europeans, 120 shillings per year

In conclusion, a breach of these new regulations is punished by death. Once you have been found guilty, you will be shot outright in the interests of the people.

Kenya Land and Freedom Army Charter

In October of 1953, in an attempt to explain the KLFA position, Kîmathi published an important document which he called the KLFA Charter. It consists of 79 articles. It was specifically addressed to the British colonial authorities in London, but, as mentioned earlier, copies of the document were also reported to have been sent to the government of India, France, Egypt; to President Eisenhower (USA), Georgi Malenkov (USSR), George Padmore (UK), Kwame Nkrumah (Ghana), Fenner Brockway UK), W.E.B. Dubois (USA), and Mbiyũ wa Koinange and Joseph Murumbi (UK).

The following is an extract from the document:

1. We want Self-Government in Kenya now.
2. We reject foreign laws in Kenya, for they are not made for Kenya and are therefore not just.
3. We demand an African Magistrate's court with full authority, which will judge us lawfully and righteously.
4. We strongly reject a foreign Attorney-General in Kenya, one who deals with appearances more than justice.
5. We reject the trial of "criminal" and "murder cases" by European judges, for we have discovered that the death penalty is used to sacrifice many of our people.

6. We want to know who handles the money paid by settlers for our land and where the money goes.
7. We reject being called terrorists for demanding our people's rights. We are the Kenya Land and Freedom Army.
8. We want to know why so many different churches have been brought to Kenya. Since there is only one God in heaven, is one Church not enough?
9. We strongly object to foreigners raping our wives and daughters, also female imprisonment and carrying passes.
10. We demand that Africans should have control of gold, markets, roads, cooperative societies and auctions.
11. We reject colonization in Kenya because it has turned us into slaves and beggars. We claim the full authority to make firearms and all other kinds of weapons without any restrictions.
12. We demand that Europeans, rascals, troops and policemen be withdrawn from Kenyan African Reserves.
13. We reject the imprisonment of KLFA cadres.
14. We oppose the dropping of poisons from the air as Europeans in Kenya are doing to Africans.
15. Our real fight is not against the white colour, but against the system carried on by the white rulers.
16. Nothing is more precious than independence and freedom. Only when we have achieved our independence can our people have genuine peace.
17. Our people will chase away the foreign exploiters, wipe out the traitors and establish an independent government of the Kenyan people.

Fraternal Solidarity and Support

Georgi Malenkov
Moscow Press
Russia

KLFA Headquarters
P.O. Box Nyandarwa
Kenya

Dear G. Malenkov,

I, Field Marshal Dedan Kĩmathi, the Commander-in-Chief of the Kenya Land and Freedom Army and the President of the Kenya Defense Council, hereby notify you and your government how cruelly we Africans are treated in Kenya, and how we are suffering under the laws of British imperialism. Under these laws, we are being killed, discriminated against, and have already been robbed of our fertile land.

Briefly, these are the political developments in Kenya:

1. The fight for political [freedom] and the hunger for land started in 1920.
2. The African's wealth—for example, cattle, goats and land—have all been taken away from him and have been shared among the British settlers.
3. The wages paid to African squatters for a month are:
    a. Woman   shs. 6.00
    b. Man   shs. 8.00
    c. Male teenagers shs. 3.00
4. An African squatter is not allowed to keep any cattle, goats or pigs except 5 to 15 sheep in the acre of land given to the family for cultivation.
5. Colour bar (racism) is the strongest weapon being used by the British rulers to govern in Kenya.

6. Kenya is a country of 245,000 sq. miles, out of that, only 3% of it is owned by Africans.

7. You will be amazed when you find out about the number of Europeans [who] occupy most of the land in Kenya, [while] Africans continue to be treated mercilessly: **a)** the British and their settler [compatriots] are: 45,000; **b)** Indian traders are: 120,000; and **c)** Africans, the real land owners are: 6.000,000.

8. When they realized how overcrowded they were, Africans became agitated, and from 1922 onwards formed political societies, many of which were banned without cause.

9. Later in 1945, after the Second World War, we formed another political body named the Kenya African Union, which was proscribed [in 1953] and its leaders exiled…after they were charged with being the directors and managers of the underground movement nicknamed Mau Mau, of which no one knew the meaning.

10. After the detention of the Kenya African Union leaders, the British declared war in the country and started killing the remaining African politicians, who then ran to the forest to save their lives. The British rulers used excessive brutality and hunted us from one village to another. They shot young militant politicians to death; they caused many young men to run to the forest, where most of them still live. The British colonialists realizing that we had escaped their first death trap, hunted to prevent us from getting food from our parents. That is when the fiercest fighting…began.

11. From that time onwards, the British colonialists began buying us…at five shillings per head to their fighting forces. (Editor's note: in order to bolster the morale of their fighting forces, each British soldier was paid five pounds for each African he killed. The African soldier was paid 20 shillings for the same job).

12. Women and girls are raped by British soldiers, who are spreading dangerous disease [which will affect] the country in [the] future.

13. Hunger has become a threat to all of us in the country, especially to the very young and the very old.

14. Africans with sticks, swords and spears are chased with rifles...bombs dropped by Lincoln [warplanes], each of which drops a bomb of 1000. The Harvard and jet pilots [are] killing defenseless Africans without concern for their age or sex.

15. No villages are left with houses; all have been destroyed.

16. In Central Province, Africans are [severely tortured], then screened and brought to one area [concentration camp] where they are ordered to live together in poor, cage-like houses, in which many deaths occur.

17. Our Generals—Matenjagwo (Gĩtaũ wa Ng'ang'a), BataBatũ and Gachuma—who first agreed to peace negotiations were killed. We therefore [insisted that] any peace negotiations [should not] take place without representatives from free nations of the world—Egypt, Russia, India, etc.

18. For and on behalf of the 6,000,000 Africans who greatly honour me, I welcome [any] support and help [from your Government]; unless you give us such help, we shall all be killed by the British who intend to inherit our land once they have killed us all. We are... sure that your intervention in this conflict will bring a ceasefire in Kenya and a happy life and a peaceful existence will return to us and to our lovely country.

19. Can you keep...silent while we are all destroyed?

20. In conclusion, I would like to assure you and your good government that there is no such thing as Mau Mau in Kenya; only a deep sea of slavery exists—a sea into which we have been dropped and [are now] struggling in.

We shall greatly appreciate any support you will offer us.
Yours,
F.M. Dedan Kĩmathi (KCAE)

Dr. Mabuyo Mugwanji
Omulamuzi
Entebbe

KENYA FREEDOM ARMY
NYANDARWA HQ
MAY 23, 1954

Dear Sir,

We, in Kenya, are horrified and terrified that the British have seen fit to depose and exile our two great Kings, namely Serete Khama and Kabaka Mutesa II. What disturbs us most is the realization that although these two great Kingdoms--Baganda and Tswana – existed before the coming of European imperialists to our continent, it is now clear that the primary aim of the British is to use all weapons [they have] to destroy them. This evil design is clear proof that the British don't want any other kingdom to exist except their own.

What I am simply asking now is this: are the Baganda going to gaze and do nothing about their exiled Kabaka? Are we going to watch passively when African Kings are deposed by foreign rulers? Is this not the time to organize our people, arm them and fiercely fight this enemy in our midst? To shed our blood for the Kabaka, for the African cause, is a big lesson for future generations.

With the support of the Kenyan people, I am ready to volunteer my forces, the Kenya Land and Freedom Army, to come there and crush the enemy forces. The Kabaka is a great African King, and we just cannot let him be dethroned and exiled without a bloody struggle. In this once connection, I am requesting the Lukiko's permission to enter Uganda; I am also requesting you to cooperate with, and support, my forces once they arrive there. Commander General Magũ, Colonel Rũanjane, and Major Mũirigo will be in charge of this army. If all goes well, they will arrive there in early June, 1954.

With your cooperation and help, we will plant a seed which will never be uprooted, and one which the coming generations will always be proud of.

In reality, our experience in Kenya has clearly shown us that the liberation of an oppressed people cannot come through prayers and tears, but through bloody confrontation with the oppressor.

The unity of our peoples is our strength.

Yours,

Field Marshal Sir Dedan Kĩmathi (KCAE)

Discipline and Unity

KLFA Directives

1. Beware of those who pretend to be intelligent. They might be dangerous.
2. Beware of Christian priests. They are leeches.
3. Discrimination in the distribution of food will weaken our unity. It should be fiercely opposed.
4. Concentrate more on fighting. Too many meetings will create disagreements and lead to disunity in our ranks.
5. We must be united in all our actions.
6. Prostitution in the revolutionary movement is a serious crime.
7. Resist tendencies toward banditry and terrorism and turn each guerrilla into a patriotic warrior.
8. Hold frequent meetings with the population in the areas of your operation.
9. Make your judgments with politeness and truthfulness.
10. Europeans are our enemy and so are all those among our people who have sided with them against our homeland.
11. Don't tell lies. Always speak the truth. Truth never perishes.
12. Don't rob or steal. Be polite to our supporters.
13. Always be interested in your revolutionary work and love your country.
14. Pray and do your revolutionary duties with vigour and determination.
15. Help one another.
16. Don't fear death because it is better to die with dignity than to live in slavery.

17. Cowards should be castrated.
18. Learn from the experience of our struggle so that you will not be cheated next time.
19. Don't be afraid of the enemy's superior weapons. We will win with courage and determination.
20. Protest the secrets of the movement with your own life.
21. Discipline is our greatest strength.

Guerrilla Camp Regulations

1. Every guerrilla camp must have a Field Secretary. His responsibility will be: to write a daily report on the camp's activities; these include: a) battles fought and all war materiel seized during the battle; b) name of guerrillas killed or wounded during the battle; c) discipline in the camp; d) social relations between guerrillas and peasants; and e) everything obtained from peasantry. The report must be sent to the KLFA Field Marshal monthly. Failure to do so will be considered a serious crime and the Field Secretary will be charged for it. No guerrilla fighter, including the commanding officer, should interfere with the secretary's work. If this happens, it should be reported to the Kenya Parliament.
2. No guerrilla should misbehave or abuse his commander. Our rule is that guerrillas should respect their commanders.
3. No guerrilla should disobey the orders of his commander.
4. No guerrilla should disclose the secrets of the movement to the enemy. The penalty for breaking this regulation is death.
5. No guerrilla should damage or spoil anything that belongs to the fellow fighter.
6. Stealing food from the kitchen or store is a crime which carries a heavy penalty.
7. Guerrillas should not abuse one another or fight one another. Any disagreement should be settled through discussions.

8. A guerrilla should not use his fellow fighter's belongings without permission.
9. To poison food or to put rounds of ammunition into the fire is an offence.
10. Every guerrilla camp must have its own hospital, foodstore and archives.
11. A guerrilla unit must construct its own gun factory.
12. Camps must always be guarded.

Secrecy and Security

A Kenya Parliament representative was strictly prohibited from being accompanied by anyone, except his main bodyguards, when attending a session of the Parliament. The Kenya Parliament Guard commandant (KPGC) was empowered to deal with such matters. For example, when Representative Kĩng'ori attended a session of the Kenya Parliament accompanied by three men in addition to his bodyguards, he was barred from attending the session by the KPGC, and was rigorously questioned about his motive for bringing the three strangers with him. What follows is discussion between the KPGC and Kĩng'ori:

KPGC: How many new men have you brought with you? [pause] Where did they come from?

Kĩng'ori: They joined me at the Rũthaithi camp. Two of them are young boys who had been abducted by Gacerũ and his men.

KPGC: Why did you bring them here and who is that third man? Where his home location and what is is his district? What is his purpose for coming?

Kĩng'ori: His home location is Mahiga, Nyũrĩ, but right now he has come from Nairobi. His name is Ndũritũ wa Theuri. I have not had a serious discussion with him about his journey here. However, he briefly told me that he had been sent by the Nairobi War Council to see the Marshal and other KLFA leaders. He mentioned some of our leaders in Nyũrĩ to whom he had written a letter asking them to await him on March 6, 1954. One of these leaders is Njango.

KPGC: Why did you bring these people here today knowing very well that the Kenya Parliament is meeting and that the Marshal and other KLFA leaders would be here? Whose fault would it be if this man tried to kill one of our leaders?

Kīng'ori: It would be my fault.

KPGC: Did you think we would believe him because you believed him?

Kīng'ori: No.

KPGC: Have you told him anything concerning our military activities?

Kīng'ori: No, I have told him absolutely nothing.

KPGC: Do you think he might be our enemy?

Kīng'ori: No, he told me that he bought 90 rounds of ammunition and sent them to General Kariba. He has also brought Shs.55.50 and one fountain pen for the Marshal. I do not think he is an enemy.

KPGC: Let him speak for himself.

Ndīritū Speaks: My name is Ndīritū wa Theuri from Mahiga Location, Nyīrī. My clan is Mūmbūi wa Mbarī ya Njogu. I am Assistant Chairman of the Mau Mau Committee, Mahiga Location. Our Chairman is Ndirangū and our Secretary-General is Wambūgū. Mathenge wa Kamotho is also a member of this committee. I also know Kīng'ori wa Kūrū, Kīmondo wa Thirikwa, and Gīthaiga wa Kīng'ori, who are fighting with General Mathenge wa Mīrūgī's force. I was one of those who persuaded them to join the armed force movement.

I came from Nairobi on March 5, 1954, by train. I got off the train at Nyīrī Station and spent a night in the P.W.D. quarters. On the following day I went to Nyīrī town to meet Gītukū. For security reasons, he took me to stay with Sosto Wambūgū from the Tetū Location, while he tried to contact the nearby KLFA unit. He succeeded to establishing contact with a

KLFA unit, and on March 9, 1954, he escorted me to General Rũi's camp. I explained to General Rũi the reasons for my journey, and he organized an armed guard to escort me to Rũthaithi.

I arrived at Rũthaithi on March 11, 1954, and met Commander Totha who is in charge of the Rũthaithi Camp. After I had rested, I told him that I would like to see Dedan Kĩmathi because I was carrying an important message for him from the War Council in Nairobi. He told me that Kĩmathi was not in the area, but he would find someone who would take me to him. And that is how I came here.

After receiving two letters from Dedan Kĩmathi (on February 20 and March 22, 1954) concerning the war situation, and in particular about the living conditions of our fighting men, the War Council resolved to send me and another compatriot from Mũrang'a here to discuss these problems with Kĩmathi and other members of the Kenya Parliament. The compatriot from Mũrang'a was refused a road pass by the colonial administration, so he could not accompany me.

The war Council wants Dedan Kĩmathi and the Kenya Parliament to know that two commissions have been established purposely to tour Nyandarwa and Kĩrĩnyaga in order to investigate the living conditions of our fighters, and also to discuss the war effort with the army commanders. One commission which is composed of eight members of the War Council from Mũrang'a and Nyĩrĩ will visit Nyandarwa, and the other one composed of eight representatives from Embu, Mĩũrũ and Nyĩrĩ will tour the Kĩrĩnyaga front.

These two special commissions were supposed to begin their investigations later December of 1953, but the money (shs. 1,000) which was set aside for this important task, together with large quantities of medicine, were seized by the enemy just a week before the commissioners started their work. Consequently, it will take some time before these special commissions are dispatched. I was also asked to explain to the Kenya Parliament that Kenyatta and other KAU leaders are no longer in Nairobi; they have been detained in Kapenguria. As a result, the possibility of rescuing them from the jaws of the enemy is almost nil.

In conclusion, I am supposed to prepare a report concerning this mission for the War council as soon as I return to Nairobi.

KPGC: Comrade Kĩng'ori, you can go and attend the Parliament, but we will detain your three friends until the session is adjourned. Do you have any objections?

Kĩng'ori: No, comrade.

Circular to KLFA Field Secretary

1. History books should contain the following information:
    a. Names of all our people who have died in this war.
    b. Names of all the people who are alive and are supporting the struggle.
    c. Record of the guerrillas' activities:

    i) Social problems
    ii) Battles fought
    iii) Names of guerrillas killed
    vi) Weapons seized by our people from the enemy

2. Document all property damaged. Destroyed or confiscated by the enemy for future compensation.

These documents should be forwarded to me or the Secretary-General of the Parliament, Karari Njama.

Marshal D, Kĩmathi
Nyandarwa, 1954

Circular to the Frontline Commanders

According to our intelligence task force, the British government will be sending a Special Commission to Kenya. This Commission will be composed of 3 members of the Conservative Party and 3 members of the Labour Party. The purpose of this commission is to investigate the causes of the war. They will stay in the country until January 31, 1954.

During their presence in the country, our job is to intensify the struggle on all fronts and kill as many enemy soldiers as we possibly can. When they go home they will tell their Queen that we mean business.

Field Marshal D. Kîmathi

Speech of Major General Chumali to his Unit

My Compatriots,

Now that we are armed, we have the greatest opportunity to help our people, to fulfill their noble aim—the liberation of this land. So we have to work hard and fast. Remember our Father Gĩkũyũ said: *"Mũthii tene akinyaga tene"* (The traveler who leaves early, arrives at his destination early).

With untiring efforts and extraordinary heroism, we will be able to change the history of this country and consequently improve the social and political life of our people. Although some of our compatriots have collaborated with the British imperialists to oppose this great national effort.

In order to succeed in this national endeavor, we must work tirelessly among the African people, teaching them the importance of our struggle, thus uniting all our forces against the foreign occupiers. Remember Kenya does not only mean Nyandarwa and Kĩrĩnyaga. It is a large country. It requires many committed cadres to go and work vigorously where our influence has not been felt. You should know that apart from the Gĩkũyũ, Embu and Mũrũ, other nationalities are determined to join the national struggle, but we haven't sent KLFA cadres to mobilize them. They want this country to be liberated, just like we do.

In this connection, each and every cadre should try to convince the oppressed masses of this land of the significance of this struggle. It is a great mistake for some of us to think that we are fighting for the liberation of central Kenya alone. (**Editor's note**: In this volume, central Kenya includes Gĩkũyũ, Embu, Mũrũ, Kamba and the great City of Nairobi.)

Finally, we should try to be concerned with, and be interested in; the political struggle of the African continent because our liberation struggle is part and parcel of the great struggle of the African peoples against world imperialism. Remember, because we dared to challenge the forces of colonialism with firearms, most people in Africa think highly of us; we have their moral and political support.

If we succeed in liberating this country from British imperialism, our people will immortalize us. We will become their great ancestors.

Nyandarwa 1953

Combat Parochialism and Chauvinism

Minutes of a Meeting of the Kenya Defense Council

Leaders Present
Field Marshal Dedan Kîmathi
Brigadier General Kahiũ-Itina
Colonel Gathitũ Waithaka
Colonel Kariũki (Makanyaga) Mathĩnji
Colonel Wambararia
Commander Abdullah Gĩtonga
Commander Ndĩritũ wa Thũita
Commander Nyaga Gathũre
Comrade Kĩbũkũ wa Theuri
General Kĩbirũ Gatũ
General Kĩmbo Mũtukũ
13 Majors
7 Captains

Importance of History

The meeting discussed how the history of the struggle should be preserved for future generations. It was collectively agreed that every army unit should have a field Secretary whose main responsibility is to document the daily activities of the guerrillas. In collecting this data, the Field Secretary will be required to use the following method:

1. Record every battle fought, including:

   a) The date the battle took place.

   b) The names of the guerrillas killed or wounded.

   c) The names of the enemy dead and the number of weapons seized by our forces.

   d) A short account of the battle.

2. Record all the property destroyed by enemy forces for future compensation.
3. List the names of the national traitors—homeguards, headmen and chiefs—in the region.
4. List the names of Mau Mau cadres and leaders in the area.
5. List the names of widows, orphans, and detained compatriots in the area.
6. This report should be sent to the Kenya Defense Council (KDC) through the Unit Army Commander.

Recruitment of Cadres

It was agreed that in order to strengthen the guerrilla army, the recruitment of youths in both the urban centers and the rural areas should be intensified. However, the leaders felt that the recruitment team must thoroughly screen potential candidates to make sure that they fulfill the ideological requirements of the movement. Only those who are conscious and brave, they stressed, should be allowed to join the armed struggle.

Desertion

The problem of desertion was seriously discussed. Some leaders, such as General Kimbo and General Kahiu-Itina, argued that desertion is the result of hunger among the fighters, and that this is why many deserters were running to the Kĩandongoro region where food is plentiful. Other

KDC members, including Kîmathi, rejected the argument and insisted that desertion is the result of indiscipline among the fighters, plus the failure of the unit army commanders to maintain firm control over their men.

To solve this pressing problem, it was agreed that deserters should be treated as war criminals and would, therefore, be punished severely.

National Treasure

Comrade Kîbũkũ wa Theuri told the meeting that there was plenty of wealth in the forest which should not be destroyed or wasted. Things like ivory and other valuable items should be documented and stored under good care until the war has been won.

Clothing Issue

General Kîmbo urged the leaders not to keep the money given to them by the War Council for themselves, but to buy clothes and other necessities for their fighting men. He pointed out that cold and rain might force guerrillas to desert.

Two Ways of Fighting

General Kahiũ-Itina told the meeting that there were two effective ways of fighting the enemy:

1. By organizing a surprise attack.
2. By ruthlessly destroying the enemy's property.

He also said that money should be distributed to army units for buying guns because guerrillas cannot fight with empty hands. In his contribution to the debate, General Kimbo said that it was about time the guerrillas learnt how to manufacture their own firearms. "We have been given wisdom by God and we must use it," he argued. "Pipes are plenty and easily obtained; I will be responsible for supplying pipes. But let us make a rule that if a certain camp does not make its own guns, its Commander will be removed from his position of leadership." In this connection, Kĩmathi said that every guerrilla leader would be required to bring the best rifle he had made to the next meeting of the Council, to be held at the end of the month. The makers of the best three guns, he said, would be rewarded.

Propaganda Unit

Commander Ndĩritũ proposed that each guerrilla column should organize its own propaganda task force, whose responsibility would be to politicize the guerrillas and counteract the enemy's false propaganda. He emphasized that war was fought through propaganda; it was therefore the duty of every unit commander to know how to use it. He also said that every unit army commander should talk with his men before and after the battle to bolster their morale. Emphasizing the significance of organizing propaganda units, Kĩmathi said that radio broadcasts were being used by our enemy in an attempt to force us to despair and lose faith in the struggle. He observed that newspapers reached us in a poor condition, and they all carried the enemy's propaganda. It was therefore necessary, Kimathi advised the Council, to have our own propaganda machine, which would be able to expose the enemy's real intention and at the same time strengthen and harden the fighting spirit of our armed forces.

Nyandarwa, December 25, 1953

Kĩmathi's Report of the Ngũthĩrũ Consultative Conference
Ref. No: EFT/3/3/542

On May 19, 1953, I was informed by Mũrũthi wa Wamathi that a young man called Ndĩritũ wa Thũita had led an attack on enemy forces at Icagacirũ Location, and that he was a brave and courageous patriot. I tried to locate his camp without success. I arrived in Mũrang'a on July 17, 1953, and on July 19, 1953, I headed for the Kĩandongoro Camp. I was fortunate enough to find comrade Ndĩritũ there, and I congratulated him for his heroism and patriotism. Subsequently, we had a serious talk about our revolutionary efforts and our lives in the forest.

The following morning, Ndĩritũ's force escorted me to the Rũhotie guerrilla camp. On the way, we had a fierce battle with the enemy forces at Kamĩgo. While Ndĩritũ's force was in pursuit of the retreating enemy forces, I was ordered to return to the Kĩandongoro Camp with immediate effect. After two days of rest, we embarked on our journey for Rũhotie. On the way, we found another bloody battle going on between our forces and the imperialist robbers. Though the enemy had tanks and other sophisticated weapons, we managed to chase them out of the region. We killed several enemy soldiers and seized their weapons; our casualties were light. I left the Rũhotie Camp on August 2, 1953, for the Chania Front to supervise the construction of a new hospital for our sick and wounded comrades.

On August 3, 1953, I received a letter from some of our war leaders, who were at the Ngũthũrũ Camp with Commander Nyaga's forces. The letter stated that Ngũthũrũ was an excellent place in which to hold a conference because it was at the center of Nyandarwa. Therefore, it would be easier for guerrillas from all parts of the forest to travel to Ngũthũrũ without alerting the enemy forces. This letter was written by Quartermaster General Macaria wa Kĩmemia on behalf of the following leaders:

1. Commander Abdullah Gĩtonga Mũthũi
2. Commander Nyaga (Mũriũki wa Gathũre)
3. General Kahiga wa Wachanga
4. General Kĩbeera wa Gatũ
5. Mbaria wa Kaniũ, Chairman of Mũrang'a armed forces
6. Senior Commander Mũraya wa Mbuthia

I agreed with their suggestion and wrote back, asking them to wait for us on August 7, 1953. At the same time, I requested them to start preparation for the conference which was to be held on August 9, 1953.

On August 6th, accompanied by Mũrũthi wa Wamathi, I returned to Kĩandongoro to inform my comrades about the Ngũthũrũ Conference. The next morning, a group of us began the journey to Ngũthũrũ. We spent the first night on the banks of the Chania River, and the following day we continued our journey to Ngũthũrũ.

About four miles from the camp, we were met by a welcoming party led by General Kībeera and Commander Nyaga. General Kībeera was carrying a calabash of honey, which, he told me, symbolized our unity in the struggle and our undying love for our country. He handed the calabash to me and asked me to drink some honey. I drank the honey from the calabash with great relish. I then suggested we move away from the road, so that we could all drink from the calabash of unity and love.

After drinking from the calabash, we prayed to *Mwene-Nyaga* and thanked Him for the historic reunion. Afterwards, General Kībeera and Commander Nyaga led us towards the camp. On our arrival, we were received with great enthusiasm, including cries of joy. For two and a half minutes, I stood in silence. "In a situation like this," I asked myself, "why should we be hunted down and be killed in our own country? Why should we live in the forest like beasts – hungry and in rags? What crimes have we committed? If fighting for our stolen land and freedom is a crime, then we shall fight to the last drop of our blood. We shall never give up until we have driven these foreign murderers from our beloved country."

After a night's rest, I sent KLFA units to Mūrang'a and Nyūrī to summon our guerrilla compatriots to the conference. Others were sent to the Rift Valley Front on a similar mission.

But on August 9, 1953, before the conference could begin, we learnt from our military intelligence network that there were enemy forces in the region. While we were discussing the important security issue, the Mūrang'a forces, led by their commanding officers –General Commander Matenjagwo, Brigadier Gakure wa Karūri and Mūraya wa Mūcerū, arrived. The following KLFA leaders also arrived at about the same time:

1. Brigadier Gathitū wa Waithaka
2. Colonel Kībirū wa Mūciiri, Field Secretary of Mūrang'a armed Forces
3. Comrade Ndirangū wa Kanoe
4. Comrade Rūbia wa Wandua

5. Karari wa Njama
6. Major Ndirangũ wa Kariũki
7. Mathenge wa Gathirũ
8. Comrade Wawerũ wa Ngĩrita, and many others whose names I cannot recall.

After consultations among the delegates, we decided to continue with the conference despite the presence of the enemy in the region. When the conference began, we discussed and criticized our war efforts; we agreed to develop a new war strategy. We also discussed the problems of promotion and discipline in the guerrilla army. At the same time, we agreed to put more efforts into combating the enemy's propaganda among the Kenyan masses, particularly the peasants. We also agreed to intensify the struggle on all fronts.

The conference approved the promotion of Ndĩritũ wa Thũita to the rank of commander for his dedication and heroism. He was transferred from his small unit and given a full battalion. Ndũrũri wa Gĩtuka was appointed field secretary of Ndĩritũ's former force. I also appointed Kĩbũkũ wa Theuri to be the coordinator of the Tetũ force and requested him to attend the KLFA general conference to give a report on his activities, but he never did.

The conference was closed after two days of tough and serious discussions. We decided that the KLFA general conference would be on August 16, 1953, at Mwathe, Nyandarwa, and that I should contact all the KLFA front commanders and the leaders of village militia.

Before winding up the conference, I requested every commander to work harder, and to make every sacrifice necessary for the liberation of our country. After these closing remarks, we parted and returned to our respective areas of operation. I left for Mũrang'a accompanied by Brigadier Gathitũ, Colonel Kĩbirũ and Comrade Ndirangũ wa Kanoe. Karari wa Njama, Kahiga wa Wachanga and Mathenge wa Gathirũ went to Nyũrĩ through Ndũndũri in the Rift Valley Province.

It was a great conference.
Nyandarwa, August 1953.

Report to the Kenya Defense Council

We moved from Thaina Camp to Kĩanjirũ where we pitched our tent. Nyaga and 40 fighters remained in the camp, while Kĩbũkũ wa Theuri and I went to Rũthaithi because I wanted to visit a guerrilla unit there.

We arrived on November 16th, but did not find any guerrillas there, they had moved out of the camp. We visited Ndũritũ wa Wang'ombe's camp where we found General Kahiũ-Itina and Colonel Gathitũ wa Waithaka, whom I had sent to prepare the KLFA expenditure account.

I spent the night there. The following morning, I visited Captain Wambararia's camp near the Ritho River. During our discussions, Colonel Wambararia reported to me that comrade Gatete had attempted to kill Comrade Juma a while back.

According to Colonel Wambararia, Gatete's undignified act had something to do with a girl, whose guerrilla name was Mũtama, from Thĩgĩngĩ Location, Nyĩrĩ.

Because of the seriousness of the matter, the KDC should appoint a special committee to investigate this incident.

Field Marshal D. Kĩmathi
November 18, 1853

Minutes of the Kenya Parliament: Ref. No. EFT/3/3/629

Karari wa Njama, the Secretary-General of the Kenya Parliament, opened the meeting by saying that we had all come to these forest to fight for our land and freedom, and if there were any members who disagreed with him, they should leave the meeting because it was obvious that they did not understand what we were fighting for. He told us that our principal aim was to gain independence for the whole of Kenya, not for Central Province alone. He clearly pointed out that our liberation struggle was closely linked with the struggle of the peoples of East Africa and the rest of the continent.

The Kenya Parliament, he continued, was the backbone of the struggle; its primary task was to guide and direct our war efforts, and to strengthen our military and political leadership. He stressed that good leadership would contribute to the improvement of the combat ability of the entire army and of every guerrilla fighter. It was therefore the duty of the members of the Kenya Parliament to work efficiently, and with great dedication. Given the fact that we were struggling under great difficulties, he continued, the KP members should become an example of courage and vigilance in the face of any hardship, be it hunger or death. If we cannot have these qualities, he said, we should quit and let other compatriots take over the leadership of the movement.

Commander Karari said that he was very concerned about disunity, disorganization and, above all, lack of discipline in the army. He pointed out, for example, that Mahiga Location and Laikipia District used to be the best organized regions because there was unity and cooperation between the guerrillas and the general population, but due to the weakness of the leadership, growing conflicts between the leading army commanders, and the influence of harmful elements within the army units in both regions, work there was no longer going smoothly, and the enemy seemed to have taken advantage of this weakness.

In this connection, Comrade Karari gave us the history of the Kariainĩ KLFA Headquarters before it was evacuated. He said that 3,500 guerrillas from Nyũrĩ, Mũrang'a, Mũrũ, Embu, Ukambani and the Rift Valley used to live there, and the peasants supplied them with food, clothing, medicine, and other important material needs. Because the leadership was firm and vigilant, there was cooperation and unity amongst the fighters. Everything, including guns, was shared communally; there existed a great spirit of togetherness and discipline that was high among the fighters. "What happened to this great spirit of togetherness? What is happening to us?" he asked.

He said that he was worried and concerned when he saw guerrilla fighters, living in one camp, unable to share things such as medicine. "If we are fighting for the same thing, if our goal is to drive the British robbers and murderers out of our country; why," he bitterly asked, "should this harmful tendency be allowed to exist?"

This dangerous trend, Karari pointed out, had been engineered by those comrades and unit commanders who preached and practiced individualism, regional chauvinism, parochialism, nepotism and disunity among the guerrilla fighters, as well as in the Kenya Parliament. These individuals are dangerous enemies of the movement and should be dealt with ruthlessly and mercilessly. When a unit commander starts talking about "I", of "my location and district", of "my army", of "my camp", he violates the rules and regulations of the Kenya Parliament and should be considered a criminal, an enemy of this great struggle; he should be severely punished, because there is no "I" in an armed struggle for our country that has been stolen by the colonialist.

Our victory, Karari concluded, depends on strong leadership in the Kenya Parliament and unity in the armed forces.

MŬRĨITHI wa GAKUŨ: In support of Karari's speech, he said that there had been discussion in his guerrilla column concerning the same issue and he was very happy that it had been raised. He emphasized the seriousness of this matter.

GĨTONGA wa GACIINGŨ: He asked Karari to explain specifically how the guerrilla camps should be organized, and how they would be run more smoothly.

Karari replied that it was difficult for him to explain exactly how guerrilla camps should be run, because each camp depended on its leadership and the concrete situation in the region it was located in. He made the following general observations:

1. Each camp must have one kitchen, headed by one person.
2. Food should be well-prepared and guerrillas should be given equal rations. However, senior ranks should be served first.

3. All utensils should be used communally. No one should have his own utensils.
4. The head of the kitchen, and not the leader of the brigade, should be responsible for the smooth running of the kitchen.
5. Women guerrillas should do the cooking and be responsible for fetching water and firewood because that is their main job. It is wrong to send men to fetch water and firewood when there are women to do it.
6. The storekeeper should be in charge of handing out food and other items to the master of the kitchen. No one else should be allowed to enter the store. In addition to the food store, the unit must build two more store—one for clothing and writing material, and the other one for war materiel and historical documents about the unit's revolutionary activities. These stores should be underground.
7. Every guerrilla base must have separate common-rooms; one for senior ranks and the one other for junior ranks.
8. The unit commander must have a separate house and should be well-guarded, because if something happened to him it would affect the morale of the entire column.
9. Women in the unit force should have separate accommodation, but they should be given equal treatment in all activities concerned with the war.
10. The camp must be guarded twenty-four hours a day. This is the responsibility of the guard commandant.
11. A war committee must be established in every guerrilla camp. It should be a military and political watchdog for the unit.
12. The camp must organize its own intelligence force. This force must work closely with the war committee and the unit's commander-in-chief.
13. A medical task force must be organized and a hospital. And the camp should be clean always.
14. Every guerrilla camp must maintain close political relations with the masses of the peasants in the area of its operation.

15. Parochialism, individualism and regional chauvinism should be fought on all levels of the unit's activities. It is the duty of the unit force to weed out harmful elements and other traitors.

16. Political and military guidelines should be followed by the unit as they are laid down by the Kenya Parliament.

17. That unit commander-in-chief should be the main force and inspiration of his detachment.

KABŨGA wa NJOGU:

He asked Karari to explain in detail how food should be distributed to guerrillas, and whether the leaders of the detachment should be given special food. On this issue, Comrade Karari said that distribution of food to the guerrillas is the responsibility of the head of the kitchen. There should not be special food for the senior ranks, but he made it clear that the senior ranks should be served first.

GENERAL KĨMBO:

To strengthen the armed struggle, he said, we members of the Kenya Parliament must trust each other, and each member, regardless of his rank and title, must accept the collective decision of the Parliament. "I am saying this because after the Parliament made the decision that any comrade who wants to see the Marshal should seek my permission first, the Marshal himself has decided to disregard this decision by allowing certain comrades to see him without consulting me," said Kĩmbo. "For instance, Comrade Karari and Commander Abdullah are with the Marshal every evening. My question therefore is this: Who has given them permission to visit him without my knowledge? Does it mean that there are those of us whom the Marshal trusts and others whom he distrusts? Isn't this supreme council weakened when its President disregards its rules and regulations? This really disturbs me."

MARSHAL D.K.:

In response to this criticism, Kĩmathi said that he was pleased with General Kĩmbo's concern about roles and responsibility in the struggle, and that he fully supported that line. He said that with the exception of Karari and Commander Abdullah who had visited him without Kĩmbo's permission, no other comrades had been allowed to see him without the General's knowledge.

GENERAL KĨMBO:

In reply, General Kĩmbo told Kĩmathi that what he seemed to have forgotten was that he was the most important personality in the liberation struggle, and that is why we were so concerned about his security. But we could only protect him from the British enemy and national traitors, Kĩmbo went on, if he, Kimathi, would accept the collective decision, the rules and regulations of the Kenya Parliament. Addressing Kĩmathi's response more specifically, Kĩmbo said: "You said that you only allowed Comrades Karari and Abdullah to see you without my knowledge, but I remember comrade Ndĩritũ wa Theuri visiting you two nights ago. If we cannot trust each other, be sincere with one another, and maintain close relations with one another, then I don't see how we can lead this great struggle." In support of General Kĩmbo, Brigadier Kĩrĩhinya, Commander Ndĩritũ wa Theuri and Major Ndũrũri criticized Dedan Kĩmathi for his actions and demanded that he accept Kĩmbo's criticism.

MARSHAL D.K.:

Acknowledging that he had been wrong, Kĩmathi said, "I accept Kĩmbo's criticism and I apologize to this body and to individual comrades for not maintaining the discipline of the movement. The error I have committed is serious. I hope I will never repeat it. I know that a lack of discipline and misunderstandings can cause serious errors in our military organization, and that is why I clearly understand and appreciate General Kĩmbo's concern."

COMMANDER NDĨRITŨ wa THŨITA:

Contributing to the debate he said that all members of the Parliament should understand that we are fighting for national liberation, for the total liberation of Kenya, and not for one nationality or region. As we continue to intensify the struggle, he said other nationalities will join us here in the forest. He went on to say that after we have kicked the British out of this country, after we have liberated our homeland, our compatriots will welcome us as national heroes; they will immortalize this glorious struggle. "With the support of the Kenyan masses, we will form the first national government under Dedan Kĩmathi's leadership," he said. In conclusion, he told us that if our primary aim is the liberation of Kenya, we should make every effort to combat chauvinism and regionalism.

MARSHAL D.K.:

In strongly supporting Commander Ndĩritũ's remarks, Dedan Kĩmathi stressed that we should use every effort, and exert all our sweat and blood, to build an invincible liberation army. Without a strong army, Kĩmathi said, we will not be able to bring the whole country under our leadership. But he said that it was difficult to build a strong and united army unless we solved the communication and transport problems, and unless we met with the army commander in Kĩrĩnyaga to coordinate our war efforts.

"As you remember," the Marshal told the Parliament, "a few days ago, I wrote a letter to General Kariba informing him of my plans to tour the Kĩrĩnyaga Front as soon as the Kenya Parliament approved my request. I am now asking the Parliament to allow me to visit the Kĩrĩnyaga Front. I think the members understand the importance of my visit. My presence will bolster the morale of our fighting forces there, and, above all, I will have an opportunity to meet General Kariba and the leaders of Embu and Mũrũ and have a concrete discussion with them on our war efforts. From there, I will travel to Nairobi to meet the members of the Supreme War council to discuss the expansion of the liberation struggle in all regions of our country."

MAJOR NDŨRŨRI:

He observed that the Parliament highly appreciated Marshal's effort to contact Army commander Kariba in Kĩrĩnyaga, but it would be a great risk to allow the Marshal to visit the Kĩrĩnyaga Front in these uncertain times. He proposed that we send another comrade instead.

Contributing to the same debate, Commander Ndĩritũ said that while he understands the seriousness of the Marshal's proposal and his intention, he strongly opposed his visit to the Kĩrĩnyaga Front because the Parliament could not guarantee his security at present. "Since you are the father and inspiration of this great movement," Commander Ndĩritũ told the Marshal, "if something happens to you it will mean the death of all of us; it will kill the struggle. No, we cannot approve your request. *Tũtingĩhe hiti tũkĩonaga* (We cannot consciously sacrifice you to the enemy"). Commander Ndĩritũ supported Major Ndũrũri's proposal that the Parliament should appoint another commander to lead the mission to Kĩrĩnyaga.

After further discussion, the Parliament rejected Kĩmathi's request, but agreed to appoint a special mission to tour the Kĩrĩnyaga Front.

Commander Ndĩritũ said in conclusion, "I hope the Marshal understands our concern and the patriotic motives which compel us to refuse him permission to tour the Kĩrĩnyaga Front.

COLONEL NDĨRITŨ wa WANG'OMBE:

Colonel Ndĩritũ pointed out that most members failed to arrive for the parliamentary session in time because of communication, transportation and security problems, whilst others couldn't come at all. This created a major problem since the Parliament couldn't meet unless two-thirds of its members are present. Since we trusted each other and we were all working for the liberation of our country, he suggested that Parliament should meet if there were only three members present. His proposal was supported by Commander Ndĩritũ wa Thũita and Colonel Ndĩritũ Omera.

Although he agreed with the sentiments of the previous speakers, Major Ndũrũri suggested that Parliament should meet if six members and the president were present. Similarly, General Kĩmbo said that to hold a parliamentary session with only three members and without the president would be unacceptable to him. He argued that if members were informed about the date for their meeting beforehand, they would certainly make every effort to arrive on time. He went on to say that the problem arose when an announcement for a meeting did not reach some members until the session had been adjourned.

The Parliament session was adjourned at 2:30 P.M.
Nyandarwa
February 1954

Minutes of the General Meeting of the Six KLFA Column under General Commander Mũthũi

Editor's Note: As mentioned earlier, every KLFA unit was required to hold a general meeting once a month to review the war situation and to discuss any social contradictions which might have occurred in the unit. The minutes of these general meetings were sent to the Kenya Parliament for examination. The following is a copy of the minutes of such a meeting sent to the Kenya Parliament by Commander Mũthũi.

A Letter of Transfer

Colonel Waciira wa Nginya's motion that any guerrilla fighter who wants to transfer to another camp must produce a letter of transfer from his original camp was seconded by three comrades. Contributing to the motion, Captain Ndĩritũ said that if a guerrilla fighter decides to join a new army unit, he should not be accepted unless he provides a letter of transfer from his unit commander. In addition to that, Major Ngũngũ observed, any unit commander who allows a guerrilla to join his column without a letter of transfer should be demoted right away. General Commander Mũthũi said that in addition to his demotion, the unit commander in question should be charged before the Kenya Parliament.

Guns and Ammunition

Speaking about firearms and ammunitions, Colonel Waciira said that the rules demanded the arming of each and every guerrilla fighter, otherwise the whole exercise would be a big joke. He said that although our main source for guns and ammunition was the enemy himself, it was the duty of each guerrilla fighter to try to make a new rifle. If he did not know how to make one, he should consult the gun experts. As for ammunition, Colonel Waciira wondered why our gun-experts had not discovered how to manufacture them.

In support of Waciira's remark, Commander Mũthũi said that a gun was a decisive element in the struggle; it should be guarded, jealously so, regardless of whether it was loaded or empty. He had noticed, he said, that there were comrades who thought that a gun was only useful when loaded. He said that this was a serious error which should be corrected.

Decentralization Programme

General Commander Mũthũi told us that the decentralization policy meant that large armies would be divided into small and equal columns. He said that armies which were unnecessarily large were difficult to organize and feed. To implement this new policy, Commander Muthui explained, our force would be divided into small brigades and it would be known as the Sixth Column. Because of these new changes, he said, there was a need to promote some of us to head these units, but he stressed that promotion depended on one's ability and revolutionary commitment. Thus, everyone should accept and respect his rank and the title he was to be given. It was also very important for lower ranks to respect higher ranks. He stressed that without military hierarchy, discipline and collective responsibility; orders could not be respected and carried out.

According to Kenya Parliament regulations, Commander Mũthũi pointed out, every KLFA battalions should consist of 2,000 men; it should also have its own war committee, whose major task would be to supervise the fighting. He explained how the members of this war committee would be chosen.

Politicization of the Masses

Commander Kĩng'ori proposed that we should continue to spread the Mbatũni Oath among the masses without violence and at the same time we should make an all-out effort to explain the aims of the movement to them. Without the support and cooperation of the people, he said, our movement would die.

Discipline, Cooperation and Unit

Captain Ndĩritũ wa Gĩtonga told us that cooperation, discipline and unity must be maintained in all guerrilla camps, and that unit commanders must be respected. In the same vein, Colonel Waciira stressed that we must obey our leaders without hesitation or complaints. When we serve food, he said, we must serve the senior ranks first. In addition, he added every camp must have a commanding officer appointed by the Army General Commander; otherwise, it would be an illegal camp. This point was strongly supported by Commander Mũthũi.

Captain Njeki said that we must help each other and work as a team. Cooperation between lower and higher ranks, he emphasized, would strengthen our position against the enemy. By helping one another, he concluded, we would be helping our fatherland. Regional Sergeant Karũga said that cooperation between the leaders and guerrillas was a must if we were to succeed in our struggle. Speaking along the same lines, Major Munyi told us that cooperation would strengthen our unity. He went on to say that we should avoid jealousy and discrimination of any kind and help each other.

Attack on Enemy

Lieutenant Major Ndĩritũ wa Kĩara said that guerrilla fighters must be well prepared during an attack, and should do whatever they are ordered to do by their commanders. They must also be disciplined and ready to move into action. Contributing to the same debate, Major Kariũki said that before we kill a compatriot who has sided with the British we should try to re-educate him, first; if he does not repent, he should be eliminated.

Construction of Guerrilla Camps

Army Commander Mũthũi said that a camp should be constructed in a strategic position and it should be guarded at all times. Sentries should be positioned a mile away in all directions. The camp must be self-sufficient in food, medicine and firearms. It must also have its own hospital. In addition to that, Captain Wathũrũra said that the camp must have its own place for storing food, medicine, clothing and war materiel. Commenting on the same issue, Commander Kĩng'ori said that the camp must have at least three stores constructed underground, some distance from the main camp.

1. The first camp must be three miles away.
2. The second one should be two miles away.
3. The third must be a mile and a half away.

He said that these stores should be manned by experts under the supervision of the unit commander.

KLFA Archives

Lieutenant Wahĩ wa Macaria proposed that we should try to preserve the history of our struggle for future generations. He advised field secretaries to record every aspect of our daily activities—battles fought, acts of individual and collective heroism, names of our compatriots killed by enemy, our general meetings, etc. In addition, he said that we should continue composing songs about the movement, which will provide documentary evidence of our struggle for use in the future.

Medicine

Commander Dr. Kĩng'ori informed us that in order to be self-sufficient in medicine, we should try to manufacture our own medicine from the leaves and roots of certain trees like our ancestors used to do. He said that any comrade who knows a particular tree which produces healing medicine should report about it to the medical unit. It was agreed that thorough research should be conducted to identify such trees.

Nyandarwa, 1954

The General Meeting of the Kĩmũrĩ Army Unit

Leaders Present

1. Brigadier Mathenge
2. Captain Irũngũ
3. Captain Mathenge
4. Lieutenant Wawerũ
5. Major Gathũra
6. Major General Vido, Chairman
7. Major Mũrũthi

Agenda

1. Improvement of our armed forces
2. Politicization of the masses in the region
3. National unity and mobilization
4. Efficiency and discipline in our ranks

5. Responsibility and good leadership in our guerrilla army
6. Protection of sick and wounded fighters
7. Problem of communication and transport

At 2:30 p.m. Major General Vido, Chief of Staff, opened the meeting. He said that he and General Commander Magũ were very disturbed about the inefficiency of the commanding officers of some columns. He pointed out that their inefficiency would no doubt disorganize and disorient the force and lower its fighting spirit. Without steel-like leadership and firm discipline in our ranks, he said, we will not wage the war successfully, and the enemy will no doubt force us to our knees. He stressed that leaders should try to reorganize their units, work together as a team, and always try to solve their political differences through discussions. This way, he noted, we would strengthen our unity and bolster our fighting morale. He said that a fierce war should be waged against opportunism, over-ambition, individualism and petty quarrels among the fighters.

Finally, he reminded us that we were the backbone of our people, and that the liberation of our country depended on us—our sacrifice and efforts. If we fail to drive the British out of Kenya, he pointed out, our people will never forgive us.

MAJOR MŨRĨITHI:

In support of Major General Vido's line, he said that leaders of a unit must learn how to work together before they try to organize others. He emphasized that unity among both low and high ranks was the cornerstone of our strength. In order to strengthen our force, he argued, past quarrels and petty-disagreement should be forgotten, and individual competition should be sacrificed to our collective spirit. He concluded by saying that beginning August 22, 1954, we should try to make an all-out effort to improve our forces.

LIEUTENANT WAWERŨ:

He said we could improve our army only if we made an all-out effort, and exerted all our energies, to bring about unity and discipline within our ranks.

BRIGADIER MATHENGE:

He said that from the time he joined the Kĩmũrĩ Army on April 19, 1954, our force had been well-organized and well-disciplined, until it was divided into three sections. He criticized the commanding generals for their inefficiency and parochialism. He pointed out that if this harmful disease was allowed to spread, it would break our unity, derail our aims and goals, thus weakening our fighting spirit. He called for the realization of our responsibilities and increased commitment and dedication.

CAPTAIN GATHŨRA:

Although he supported the previous speakers, he said that the situation was not as bleak as the majority of them had presented it, that the fighting morale of the army was excellent, and we had excellent relations with the peasants. What worried him most, he said, were our communication and transport problems. He suggested that we appoint a task force to deal with these problems; otherwise they would hamper our progress.

Finally, the meeting attendees agreed that it was the duty of the army and of every guerrilla to defend sick and wounded comrades from enemy attacks.

Major Vido adjourned the meeting with the following prayer:

O *Mwene-Nyaga*,
We know that thou chooseth good things
Which last forever
We trust and believe in you dearly

Because of your greatness and kindness
I beseech you to give us wisdom and power
That will make us acquire our land
And enable us to lead our compatriots
From this colonial madness to freedom, justice and happiness

O Mwene-Nyaga

You know how the Europeans hate, oppress and exploit us
Give us strength to drive them into the sea
To drive them out of this our country
In the name of our ancestors—Gĩkũyũ and Mũmbi
We beseech you
Thai Thathaiya Ngai
Thaai

    Nyandarwa
    August 22, 1954

Commander Ndĩritũ's Report to his Unit on the Meeting of the Kenya Parliament

After returning from the session of the Kenya Parliament, Commander Ndĩritũ called us to report the proceedings of the meeting. He began his report by telling us how well the meeting had been attended. The leaders who attended included the Supreme Commander of the Kenya Land and Freedom Army, Marshal Dedan Kĩmathi. For this season, he told us that he would only tell us what he had been authorized to disclose by the Marshal and the Kenya Parliament.

1. He said they discussed the reorganization of the entire armed forces. The KP members felt that in order to make it effective and strong; the guerrilla army must be decentralized and be reconstructed into small solid columns. Each column would be led by an experienced guerrilla leader. Each Army Commander, he said, would be responsible for the

implementation of this policy and the selection of leaders for these new columns.

2. To implement this policy, he told us, our unit would have to be divided into three equal columns, since it was unnecessarily large. This process would be accomplished through democratic discussion amongst the guerrilla fighters, and discrimination and favoritism would not be allowed to hamper these new changes. In this regard, the rules and regulations of the liberation army would have to be followed to the letter; nothing contrary to these rules would be done:

   a) Each column must establish its base and organize a medical task force to take care of the sick and wounded comrades. In addition, it must be self-sufficient in food, etc.

   b) Each column must follow the rules and regulations of the movement and a steel-like discipline must be maintained and enforced with firmness.

3. He pointed out that the Marshal was seriously concerned with petty quarrels and disagreements in various guerrilla camps, and that he had ordered us to stop these divisive activities with immediate effect. He said that if someone was annoyed with a particular person, he should have a peaceful discussion with that individual instead of blaming everybody. There is no purpose to having guerrilla fighters in one camp if they cannot work together.

4. If a leader or an ordinary guerrilla fighter wants a period of rest, he told us, it should be granted; however, the leader must make sure that someone is performing his duties during his absence. To take a vacation without permission is a crime punishable by death.

5. Finally, Commander Ndĩritũ asked Karũũ wa Gĩthũmbĩri to give us a report on the war efforts on the Kĩrĩnyaga Front. Karũũ spoke well of the place. He said that the guerrilla army in the area was well-organized and well-disciplined; each guerrilla commander was responsible for drawing up a war strategy for the area in which his army unit operated.

The commander was also responsible for developing good relations with the peasantry in the region. Furthermore, he said that promotion was regarded as a very significant thing, and that only those who had proved their heroism would be promoted. He regarded Generals Tanganyika and Kariba as the best Mau Mau strategists.

In closing the meeting, Commander Ndĩritũ said that if we worked with determination and displayed exemplary heroism, we would be able to liberate the country within a year.

Nyandarwa
June 17, 1954

Report: Punishment of Deserters

The following five guerrillas were tried in Marshal D. Kĩmathi's court on November 25, 1954 for desertion, and for committing rape. As a result, they were sentenced to be caned as shown below:

1. Karũhĩ Mũthami: 15 strokes
2. Kĩnguru Ngaoba wa Kĩbogoro: 5 strokes
3. Kĩraikũ M. Wanjiri wa Theuri: 10 strokes
4. Mũkungi Mũkemi wa Gĩthanga: 5 strokes
5. Mũnũari Ndũng'ũ wa Wandete: 10 strokes

Since discipline is the most important weapon in this struggle, it must be strictly observed. We can win this war only if we have the support of the population.

Comradely yours,
Gathitũ wa Waithaka
KDC General Secretary
November 1954

Report on Kĩmathi's Visit to Icagacirũ

On April 3, 1954, at about 4 pm, we began our journey to Icagacirũ. A party of about 150 strong was escorting the Marshal. When we arrived at Gakanga, Commander Ndĩritũ ordered Major Mũirigo to organize an armed escort to protect the Marshal and his party from a possible surprise enemy attack. Some took their position in the front and some in the rear. It was a good journey.

On the way back, we composed a new fighting song which was sang with vigilance and determination:

>When we arrived at Icagacirũ
>The peasants gave us food
>And slaughtered a ram
>As rations for our mission
>
>We were happy as we went
>We were happy as we returned
>Our mission was a victory both ways
>
>When we arrived at the Chania River
>Kĩmathi commanded boldly
>"Put your guns in position
>The enemy is approaching"

Before we reached the fringe of forest, Kĩmathi decided to visit his home village. So Major Mũirigo ordered comrade Gĩtekobe to proceed with a few armed guerrilla commandos in order to check the movement of the enemy forces.

We passed by Dedan Kĩmathi's house, where he was enthusiastically greeted by peasant women. Some wept with resentment and anger when they remembered the price set on his head by the colonialists.

It was a moving scene.
Karari Njama
Chief Secretary

Reorganization of the Kenya Inooro Army

The following leaders have been sent by the Kenya Parliament to Kĩambu for an important mission:

1. Acting Commander Rũirũ wa Gacerũ—Tetũ, Nyĩrĩ
2. Captain Gathũmbĩri wa Kamau—Gĩthũngũri, Nyĩrĩ
3. Major Kahiga wa Gateri—Rwathia, Mũrang'a
4. Major Ndirangũ wa Kariũki—Tetũ, Nyĩrĩ

Purpose of their Mission

a) To administer the Batũni Oath in order to establish unity with the people behind the armed movement.

b) To recruit more youths into the guerrilla army.

c) To reorganize the Kenya Inooro Army and to establish its headquarters in the district.

As freedom fighters, we must realize that we are fighting for the whole of Kenya. There are some of our comrades who place their location or district above our country; there are others who naively think that we are only fighting for the freedom of Central Province. This incorrect line must be combated vigorously. Our people are being killed, tortured, raped and convicted because they are demanding land and freedom, because they want our country to be free.

We must remember that we are only a small [nationality] among all Kenyan [nationalities], and our actions will be remembered forever if they are good and patriotic.

Marshal D. Kĩmathi
Nyandarwa 1954

Report on our Mission to Kĩambu: Ref. No. EFI/3/3/650

We started our journey from the Honi River in Nyandarwa; we were twenty guerrilla fighters who had been sent by Field Marshal Kĩmathi wa Waciũri to politicize the masses in Kĩambu in the name of Gĩkũyũ and Mũmbi.

After walking for twelve miles, it started raining heavily and we were soaking wet. Captain Wang'ombe wa Mwangi suggested that we should make a fire to warm ourselves, but this suggestion was turned down. We decided to proceed with our journey despite the rain and cold. At about 1 p.m., we rested and ate our lunch. Then we started off, and after walking half an hour, we saw two rhinos grazing across the path we were following. Commander Waihwa wa Theuri tried to force them to move from our path, but they resisted violently. To avoid a dangerous confrontation, Commander Waihwa commanded us to go back and try to find another path, but the beasts followed us; they were ready for a fight. They troubled us for half an hour before we managed to escape. We could have gunned them down with our machine guns, but KLFA's rules prohibited the killing of animals unless it was for food.

It was still raining heavily, and it was about 1 a.m. when we decided to find a place to sleep. Luckily, the path we followed led us to a guerrilla camp, and after the Guard Commander was satisfied that we were not enemy soldiers, he welcomed us to the camp. The fighters in this camp were operating in North Kinangop under General Mũraya.

The guerrillas made a fire for us and gave us some food. After a long and comradely conversation, they showed us where to sleep. After sleeping for two hours, we woke up. We said goodbye to our comrades and we left. Since our guide did not know the way from the camp, the unit commander ordered two of his men to guide us. After escorting us for a distance, the comrades returned to their camp. At about 3 p.m., we rested and ate our food. We then continued on with our journey until we were completely exhausted; then we decided to rest. We lit a fire and warmed our food. We ate and then went to sleep. It was very dark.

We took off early the next morning. As we were crossing the South Kinangop plains at about 3 p.m., we met two of our comrades whose guerrilla unit was based in this region. They gave us some information on enemy operations in the area, and then we parted. After walking for four days, we reached a small town called Kĩnyahwa, located in a European's plantation. From there onwards, 28 miles of plains lay ahead of us, and we had to hurry to avoid detection by the enemy at dawn. We started crossing this plain about 3 a.m., but unfortunately the place we were supposed to hide had been burned down by the enemy and our contacts had been arrested. Consequently, we spent the whole day lying on the grass; we could not stand or sit up for fear of being discovered by the enemy. Despite these difficulties, we were determined to fulfill our mission, to contribute our sweat and blood for the liberation of our country.

We started off again in the evening, but because we were hungry and exhausted, we could only cover ten miles of the plain before we were forced to rest. The following morning, we sent out scouts to see whether the way was safe. We started off again when they returned, but despite our courage and determination, we could hardly walk this time; we were too hungry and tired. It was under these difficult circumstances that one of our comrades, Kamwamba, went out and brought back some honey, which saved us from starvation. We started our journey again and managed to reach Mũnyũ Railway Station at about 5 a.m. We took cover by the roadside.

We knew that some loyalists delivered their milk to the station during this time of the day and we were determined to use whatever means necessary to seize some of their milk. At about half past six, we saw one loyalist bring milk to the station on a donkey. Commander Waihwa gave the order, we captured the man and seized his milk and everything else he had in the name of our struggle. The chap looked so frightened and shocked that we decided not to kill him; but we made it very clear to him that if he reported this incident to the colonial authorities we would find him and cut him down. We released the bastard after giving him a good beating. We drank the milk, released the donkey, and then we left the station, following the tarmac road for 20 miles. A car passed us almost every five minutes, and we were instructed to lie down by the roadside to avoid detection. However, one comrade, Mbũrũ wa Njũrainĩ, had not been following these instructions, as we discovered the following morning. Commander Waihwa was furious about it.

After walking for 15 miles, we saw some cattle lying by the roadside and decided to kill one for food, but Comrade Kĩmani wa Kahora advised us not to do so for own safety; we took his advice.

We were Given Friendly Welcome at Thwariga's Camp

The whole journey from Nyandarwa Mountains to Kĩambu took us six days. We arrived on the night of August 16, 1954. The following morning, we entered Lari Forest and since we were dead tired, we decided to rest. After we had rested, it was decided that two comrades—Major Mũhĩnjũ and Kamanga—who knew the area well, would go out to survey the situation and also try to find ways of obtaining food. For security reasons, the rest of us remained in the forest until our two comrades returned. They shortly returned accompanied by another comrade called Captain Thwariga, who took us to his camp where we were given a tremendous welcome by his men. We remained in that *mbuci* (camp) from 17 to 31 August

Thwariga was very kind to us during this period. He was particularly happy to hear that Dedan Kĩmathi had sent us to Kĩambu to politicize the masses, and to help in the reorganization of the Kenya Inooro Army. At first he had suspected us of being members of the Moscow Society, but after questioning us carefully he was satisfied that we were not the enemies of the movement. In fact, Captain Thwariga organized a meeting with the leaders of the Mau Mau movement in the area, so that we could explain the purpose of our mission more concretely. The meeting was held some distance from Thwariga's main camp.

Captain Wang'ombe spoke on our behalf. He explained the primary aims of our mission with great clarity. The leaders asked him many questions, to which he replied to the best of his ability. Since it was too late for the leaders to go back to the village, they stayed with us until the following morning. When we parted, they promised they would do everything possible to make our mission successful.

Two days after we returned to Thwariga's camp, we were attacked by enemy forces. The battle continued until late in the evening. When the enemy retreated, we held an emergency meeting. We decided to divide our large force into small columns in order to defend our position effectively, if and when the enemy returned. Our group, which had 20 people, was ordered to go to the Kĩrangi camp for protection. However, Captain Wang'ombe was unable to come with us because he was having pain in his knees; he had been wounded twice during the battle. He remained with Thwariga's column.

Next morning, as expected, the enemy deployed its forces in the whole region. Peasants were beaten, tortured and killed with incredible brutality by the enemy soldiers. Many peasants were arrested and detained. Meanwhile, our column was intercepted by the enemy before it could reach the Kĩrangi camp. It was a fierce battle, but the enemy was able to force us to scatter. The majority of men in our group returned to Thwariga's camp and a few, including Commander Kĩmani, headed on for Nyandarwa. They joined up with Mũrang'a guerrillas who were operating on the border region.

Captain Thwariga and another comrade had gone to survey the situation, but unfortunately, they were ambushed and killed by the enemy. We lost a real comrade. Thwariga was a real patriot. He died a martyr.

We remained in Thwariga's camp for four days. On the fifth day, Major Mũhĩnju ordered us to go to Kĩrangi to try to find the rest of our comrades. We were guided by those guerrillas who knew the area well.

On arrival at Kĩrangi, we joined up with General Nũbi's force. General Nũbi led a group of fierce guerrilla fighters who never slept if they heard that the enemy was in the region. At any rate, after two days in the camp, Commander Nūbi, Mūhīnju and Gatimū decided to go out and fetch some food. They went out for two days. Before they could get the food, they had to wage a fierce war battle with some of the homeguard traitors, killing several of them. After forcing these traitors to flee, they broke into a shop and loaded everything into the truck they had seized; then General Nūbi drove it to the forest edge, unloaded the food and burned the truck. They brought plenty of food for the camp. There was a great joy in the camp where there was nothing left to eat.

At this time, we learned that the enemy was planning an attack on our camp. We were prepared for it; when it came, we stood our ground. We killed twelve of the enemy soldiers and forced the rest to flee. We suffered two dead and two wounded. Despite the deaths of two of our comrades, we were very happy because we had won the battle and seized guns and ammunition.

After the first battle, however, the enemy poured reinforcements into the region; we decided to leave for Longonot to escape from their deadly weapons. Captain Kanyenye was leading us when, after only five miles, we met the enemy coming to guard the path we were following. But it was pitch dark, and we were able to cross the tarmac road without being seen by the enemy. On the side of the highway, there was a maize *shamba*; we loaded some green maize into the bags and took them with us. At about 2 o'clock in the morning, General Nūbi gave us permission to light a fire and cook; after eating, we slept. At about 5 a.m., Major Mūhīnju woke us up to pray and to begin preparations to climb the mountain. We climbed up to Kīhīko's camp, which had been in existence for a long time. Kīhīko's men welcomed us and gave us food. After eating, we were informed that the commander, comrade Kīhīko, had returned from Nyandarwa and was on his way to the Kīrangi Camp with 140 guerrillas. We sent him a message and he came back. Although we still had to watch for the foreign enemy, our main immediate enemy was lack of water. There was no water on the hill. Under these circumstances our woman seer advised us that if we sacrificed another goat for food, it would definitely rain. We killed a goat before for the same purpose, but it had not rained because, according to the seer, a mistake was made during the ceremony. This time was managed to kill two goats one to replace the first sacrifice and the other for purification. The ceremony was performed on November 6, 1954. On the same night, a star was seen shooting from east to west, and the following day it rained heavily. We had enough water to drink.

On November 11, 1954, we were attacked by enemy aircraft from 6 o'clock in the morning until 12 noon. During this attack, we lay on our stomachs to avoid being seen by murderous pilots. A funny thing happened during the attack; Major Kĩbuthia ran and lay on the legs of the comrade seer. He pressed her legs so hard that she had to move from that position although the air attack was still on. As an old woman, she felt that it was indecent for a young man to lie on her legs.

The problem with Longonot Mountain is that it has no trees, so we had a rough time trying to hide from the jet bombers, but thanks to our God, none of our men were hurt. After the aircraft left; we changed our position and went further up the mountain. While we were doing this, an enemy scout plane circled the mountain; it appeared so suddenly that we thought we had been spotted. Under these dangerous circumstances, General Nũbi ordered us to change our position again and we went two miles away from our previous position. But all of a sudden, we saw the enemy coming up the mountain on foot from all directions. Army Commander General Karii ordered us to get our guns and prepare for battle.

We had sick comrades up on the mountain and, knowing the barbarity of the enemy, we were really worried. In this tense situation, Comrade Nyamũndĩtũ and Captain Wanjirũ volunteered to risk their lives to save our sick comrades. They crept with steel-like determination up to the place where the sick fighters were until they manage to bring them down safely to us. The whole operation took two hours and a half.

We decided it was not tactically wise to stage a battle with the enemy, and we managed to leave the area under cover of darkness. We marched towards Lari forest, and after four days, without food or water, we joined up with Captain Thwariga's former brigades, now under Captain Kĩhia. Altogether, we were now 368 men. We stayed in Kĩhĩa's camp for six days and we had plenty to eat. At the same time we were able to organize successful attacks against the British forces and the Kenyan traitors.

On the seventh day, we decided to go to the Kĩrangi Camp in order to hold a meeting with peasant women. Quartermaster Lieutenant Mũriũ was chosen to lead the force. He ordered the guerrilla guard to go ahead of us. But when we arrived at the camp, we discovered that our guards were dead – killed by the enemies of our people.

The brutal murder of our comrades was clear proof that the enemy was in the region and that we should expect a surprise attack any time. We had some peasant women with us who had taken refuge in the forest to escape the homeguard's brutality. We were worried about their safety. Captain Kĩhĩa, who had escorted us to Kĩrangi, sent out a guerrilla detachment to check the movement of the enemy; suddenly the enemy surrounded us from all sides, and we were forced to evacuate the base and also to change our strategy. In accordance with the decision of our commanders, we divided ourselves into small columns in order to escape the enemy's encirclement.

I was in a group of nine comrades, under Captain Kĩhĩa's command – five women and four men – and several peasant women who were MM members; after a fierce battle we were able to break through the enemy's encirclement; and then we walked for two miles without resting. In fact, Captain Kĩhĩa and Comrade Mũrũa wa Wanjirũ wanted to go and study the situation without resting, but their request was unanimously rejected because it was too dangerous to walk alone when the enemy was everywhere.

At about 6 p.m., Captain Kĩhĩa issued orders to S. S. Major Mũhĩa to lead us to a safe hideout where we could at least rest peacefully. In the meantime, the women comrades were given orders to collect firewood. Whilst collecting the firewood they met Comrade Wanjikũ who had disappeared during the battle; we thought they had killed her. We rejoiced on seeing her again. We went to sleep after warming ourselves around the fire. We had no blankets, but you know we had become used to the cold and other harsh conditions of these forests. In the morning, we prayed to *Mwene-Nyaga* as usual, seeking His support in the struggle.

Around 10 o'clock in the morning, S.S. Major Mũhĩa was sent out with armed guards to study the situation. They came back at about 12 o'clock and informed us that the enemy was nowhere to be seen. At 4 p.m., Captain Kĩhĩa ordered us to go out and get some food; we had not eaten for two days. Quartermaster Lieutenant Mũrĩu was ordered to go ahead of the column with a small well-armed detachment. With Captain Kĩhĩa in front and Captain Mũrũa wa Wanjikũ at the rear, we followed Lieutenant Mũrĩu from a distance.

Because we had some old women with us, we were going slowly. And before we had gone a mile from our hideout Lieutenant Mũrĩu and his men were suddenly attacked by the enemy; after an intense engagement, the enemy fled. Knowing the ruthlessness and savagery of the enemy, we felt it was better for us to return to our hideout until we were very sure of the situation. However, our women comrades disagreed with this decision and instead insisted that we continue. "*Gũkũ nĩ gwitũ*," they said, "*tũtigĩkua makĩrĩaga.*" ("This is our country; we cannot die of starvation while they feed.") We fought the enemy as we went along and it was not until two days later that we reached a farm where we could gather green maize and sweet potatoes. We then returned to our temporary camp still amazed by the brave stance the women had taken. We felt that with this kind of heroism, the British occupiers would have to quit this country, come what may.

On the following day, we were reunited with other fighters from whom we had been separated four days ago. They informed us that they had lost one comrade during the fierce battle. However, they were happy because they managed to force the enemy to leave the region. They also informed us that a detachment from the Lari camp was looking for Captain Kĩhĩa and the women. We were happy to hear all this, and we immediately began our journey to Captain Kĩhĩa's camp. We arrived safely, and we were informed that the situation was under control in the region. We ate, and sang revolutionary songs throughout the night. Listen to the following stanza:

> Ona twathĩnio na kana tũragwo
> Tũtigatiga kwaria
> Tũtarĩ na gwakũrũma irio
> Na wĩyathi witũ kĩũmbe
> Bũrũri witũ mwega Kenya

> Even if we are tortured and killed
> We shall never be silence
> Without land to cultivate
> And our own freedom
> In our beloved country of Kenya

On November 29, 1954, Captain Wang'ombe and Comrade R.S. M. Njagĩ wa Gĩtarĩ insisted that we return to Nyandarwa Mountains in order to attend the KLFA Conference. Consequently, we decided that 16 Kĩambu comrades should remain behind to continue our war efforts and four of us would return to Nyandarwa to report our mission to the KLFA Supreme Commander, Field Marshal Dedan Kĩmathi.

Accompanied by Major Gĩcaga wa Njũgũna's force, we started our journey to Nyandarwa. We were under Captain Kĩhĩa's command. We arrived at the Longonot Camp in the morning. December 1, 1954, and we were given a comradely welcome by our compatriots. We shared the food we had; after eating, we discussed the seriousness of our revolutionary struggle. We said goodbye to Captain Kĩhĩa and the rest of our comrades at about 8 p.m., and headed for Naivasha with Major Gĩcaga's force as an escort. As soon as we reached the foot of the mountain, it started to rain heavily. When it stopped, we marched to Longonot town. As we approached the town, we split into two groups. One group went to the Railway Landhies and the other went to the P.W.D. quarters. Although the enemy had put watchlights around the town, our compatriots, members of the movement, were not afraid; they came out in large numbers to welcome us. After receiving some food and explaining the purpose of our mission, we left. We arrived at Mũnyũ Camp on December 2 at 7 am. The camp was under the command of Colonel Kibe wa Kĩmani. We were given a big welcome by our comrades-in-arms. They slaughtered two cows for us. The cows had been seized from a European's farm in the area.

On December 4, Major Gĩcaga's force returned to its base in Lari Forest. We stayed in Kibe's *mbuci* for two weeks. On the 13th of December, we met Army Commander Gĩcũkĩ wa Mwai and agreed to hold a meeting at his camp on the 15th of December, in order to explain the purpose of our mission. The following guerrilla leaders attended the meeting:

1. Captain Mĩrũgĩ wa Karanja
2. Captain Wang'ombe — Nyĩrĩ
3. Captain Wangware — Kĩambu
4. Colonel Kibe wa Kĩmani — Kĩambu
5. Commander Gĩcũkĩ — Nyĩrĩ
6. Comrade Kĩrĩro wa Mũgaca
7. General Kĩhara — Nyĩrĩ
8. Lieutenant Gĩkuhĩ — Nyĩrĩ
9. Lieutenant Mwanangi
10. Major Marang'ũ — Mũrang'a
11. Major Matheri — Kĩambu
12. Major Mũigai — Kĩambu
13. R. S. Major Njagĩ — Nyĩrĩ
14. Sergeant Major Shida — Kĩambu
15. Sergeant Njoroge — Kĩambu

The meeting was addressed by Captain Wang'ombe, General Commander Kĩhara and Commander Gĩcũki. The guerrillas were pleased with what the speakers said; they were especially glad to know that there was to be a KLFA General Conference in Nyandarwa on the 23rd of December, and that they had been invited to send a delegation. In connection to this, they selected the following commanders to be their representatives at the Conference:

1. Captain Gĩkuhĩ
2. Captain Mũrũgĩ
3. Captain Wangware
4. Colonel Kibe wa Kĩmani
5. Commander Kĩhara
6. Comrade Kĩrĩro
7. Lieutenant Mwanangi
8. Sergeant-Major Shida

The meeting ended at about 5:30 p.m. The following day, we left for Kibe's camp. On December 17th at about 6 p.m., after saying goodbye to our comrades-in-arms, we left for Karatĩ at about 8:30 p.m., we were crossing Njabinĩ plains. We entered Nyandarwa Forest at about 9:45 p.m., and after eating we slept. The following day, we tried to find those of our comrades who operated in the region without success. When we got water, we prepared our meal and slept.

On December 19th we headed for the Mũgũra Camp. The region was so hilly that we were completely exhausted when we arrived there. It was late in the evening and since we were so tired, we prepared our meal and went to sleep. The following day, as we were busy searching for a guerrilla camp in the region, we saw footprints. Since we were not sure whether they were the footprints of the enemy or of our comrades, the Commander Kĩhara ordered two commanders, Captain Wangware and Gĩcerũ wa Mũkuro, to find out whether they belonged to our people. At about 11:25 a.m., they came back accompanied by two elderly guerrillas. They were thoroughly questioned by Commander Kĩhara. After he was satisfied that they were our comrades-in-arms, he ordered us to give them food. They told us that their camp was a mile and a half away, and that they had been sent out by their camp commander to look for food.

After we parted with the two guerrilla comrades, Commander Kĩhara and Comrade Kĩrĩro went out to look for a good hideout for us to sleep in; soon after Comrade Kĩrĩro returned and ordered us to follow him. After crossing the Mũrũga and Gakuru Rivers, we found Commander Kĩhara at a deserted guerrilla camp. We figured that it had been attacked by the enemy soldiers and that was why it had been abandoned. We decided not to sleep there for security reasons; we moved to another place.

On December 21, 1954, we started on our last leg for Mĩhuro in Nyandarwa where the KLFA General Conference was scheduled to be held. After walking for 45 minutes, we reached a place called Mĩrango ya Nderi. Since Captain Wang'ombe and R. S. M. Njagĩ knew this region very well, they were ordered to be our guides. We reached Mĩhuro late in the night, and after eating our meal, we slept. At 10 a.m., Captain Wang'ombe, accompanied by two comrades, went out to try and find out where the conference was taking place. After a while they came back and asked us to follow them. When we reached the place where the conference was being held, we met Field Marshal D. Kĩmathi, Army General Commander Abdullah, and other prominent KLFA Generals. We were very happy to join them. In the meantime, we introduced the eight Naivasha comrades who had accompanied us, and then we were given an enthusiastic welcome complete with patriotic songs.

When we gave the account of our journey to the conference, we were given a tremendous applause. We were personally congratulated by Field Marshal D. Kĩmathi for our noble, revolutionary work.

PART THREE
There Will Be No Compromise

Letters to the Colonial Authorities

An Open Letter to the British Authorities

Dear Sir,

After taking a long journey, travelling throughout Africa and Palestine for three months, I have found that many things have changed, and evil has increased a great deal. For the return of peace and the birth of a new Kenya, I have told all leaders of my army in the forest to stop fighting from August 1, 1953. General Kahiũ-Itina, who is a special leader, is now under arrest for attacking Kagũndũinĩ, the Tetũ Location of Chief Mũhoya wa Kagumba of Nyĩrĩ, without my permission. We want peace, but we maintain that we must first be recognized as a people. We will always find food despite your efforts to stop us from getting it.

As a member of the Defense Council of the whole of Africa, and the President of the branch in Kenya, I ask the [Colonial] Government to withdraw all its forces, including the police and the KAR troops from all areas of our country and stop the European settlers from hunting in the forest, then fighting will cease and racial cooperation will be established. I am telling you, very clearly, that there is no Mau Mau; since the poor man is Mau Mau, it is only Mau Mau, which can finish Mau Mau, not bombs and other weaponry.

Because of the [Colonial] Government's policy of moving people without any consideration, and of harassing them in the Reserves, many people have come to the forest for fear of being killed or badly beaten. As a result, Mau Mau has increased a thousand times and now I am glad that I have many soldiers.

When KAU (Kenya African Union) was proscribed, I congratulated the [Colonial} Government because I received many *askaris*. Many Africans who were confined in Nairobi said they had been given a good reason to follow me in the forest. Every week and every month, I received many people in my office coming from Nairobi, Nakuru and other small towns.

1. If people are being wantonly attacked in the towns and even in the reserves, how can they put up with it without running into the forest?
2. If the police and KAR and homeguards withhold food, then who can put up with hunger?
3. If there is no political organization here in Kenya, why should everyone not side with Mau Mau?
4. If colour discrimination continues in Kenya, will the Africans, who have eyes, ears and a brain, remain the underdog?
5. It is better to die than to live in misery; why should we put up with suffering in our hearts [and in our own country]?

Now it is the responsibility of the the [Colonial] Government to see whether [what I have said is] true or not. The foundation of lawful cooperation is also the foundation of peace, wealth and progress.

Why should the [Colonial] government not believe me? I am certain after next month, it will.

Yours,
Field Marshal Dedan Kîmathi

Editor's note: A copy of this letter was sent to the editor of ***Habari za Dunia*** for publication. The letter reached the editor, W.W.W. Awori, on Monday, August 26. 1953. On the following day, he handed it over to the police. Speaking to the *East African Standard* about the letter, Awori said:

It is the only [letter] we have received from Dedan Kîmathi. I am sure the signature is authentic because I know the writing. Kimathi was at one time a branch secretary of the Kenya African

Union. The letter was dated 14 August, and is written with a ballpoint pen. The address appears to be the Ihūrūrū Location of Nyīrī. It was delivered through normal post office channels, and although the franking on the envelope is not very clear, it appears to be Nyĩrĩ. I have been wandering whether it is a copy of a letter sent to the Governor, but I am not sure. I cannot understand the use of the date 1 August, as the date to end the fighting, [and even] his reference to the defence council of all Africa is an enigma to me, as is his visit to Palestine.

The colonial newspaper, the *East African Standard*, published a distorted copy of this letter on August 28, 1953.

The District Commissioner   May 21, 1954
P.O. Box 32
Nyeri

Dear Sir,

This is to inform you that if the [Colonial] Government wants to communicate with me about a peace settlement, it should do so through my mother. The communication should be given to Senior Chief Mūhoya, who will pass it to Headman Joshua Wakabe, who will then hand it personally to my mother. This is one of the ways by which I can be contacted.

The other way to communicate with me is to organize a special letter box near the liberated territory which we could use as a point of contact. However, if your government wants to write to me directly, my address is:

Field Marshal Sir D. Kĩmathi (KCAE)
GMK Ngobo Office
P.O. Karūri
Ngamune

Please inform the [Colonial] government officials, particularly the British Commander-in-Chief, General George Erskine about this communication.

To make my position clear, peace can be restored in this lovely land only if your government withdraws its armed forces from our country unconditionally.

Best regards,
D. Kĩmathi

Sir Frederick Crawford
Acting Governor of Kenya
P. O. Secretariat
Nairobi

A.G. M. Chumali
P.O. Box 32
Nyeri
May 23, 1954

Dear Sir,

The consistent murder of unarmed Kenyans, the administration of an anti-Mau Mau oath to the peasants in central Kenya and the Rift valley, the imposition of a dusk-to-dawn curfew throughout the country, the confiscation of our livestock, the burning of our homes, and the destruction of the crops in the field, is clear evidence that the principal intention of your government is to use atrocities to force our people to submit to your inhuman rule.

To put it in simpler language, we consider you, the Chief Native Commissioner, PCS, DCs, and the colonial chiefs, as our principal enemy, and we will make every effort to destroy you.

Finally, we want to make it clear that the majority of our people support Mau Mau against your government, which is based on oppression and exploitation.

A. G. M.
Copy to:
Hon. E.M. Mathu
Hon. W.W.W. Awori
Chief Native Commissioner

Corrections: A dusk-to-dawn curfew was only imposed in the central region and the European occupied areas of the Rift Valley province where fighting was heavy.

The Magistrate P.O. Box 32
Supreme Court Nyeri
P.O. Box Nairobi May 28, 1954

Dear Sir,

I, A.G.M. Chumali, hereby file a case against the persons whose names appear below for being the managers and organizers of an unlawful oath ceremony. The accused have set up an unlawful society whose aims are to engineer civil war amongst the Agĩkũyũ.

The names of the accused are:

1. C. F. Alkins, DC
2. E.A. Sweatman, PC, Southern Province
3. George Erskine, the C-in-C
4. Mr. Johnstone, PC, Central Province
5. R.E. Wainwright
6. Sir Frederick Crawford

Kindly send the forms to file the case. Names of witnesses will insert on the forms when they are received.

Yours sincerely,
A. G. M. Chumali

Editor's note: The anti-Mau Mau oath campaign was the brainchild of Lord Delamere. It was endorsed by a white settler's conference which was held in Nakuru on January 20, 1953. The pro-colonial newspaper, the *East African Standard,* states:

A delegate conference of white settlers, at a meeting at Nakuru, today adopted a plan to try to settle the Kenya emergency by making all [Gĩkũyũ] employees swear an oath of loyalty to the Queen.

The suggestion was made by their chairman, Lord Delamere, who was presiding over a meeting of the recently formed United Kenya Protection Association.

Lord Delamere suggested that within the next three weeks every employer of Gĩkũyũ labour in the settled areas should hold meetings which should be attended by a Resident Magistrate. The meetings would be formal, with the Union Jack and a picture of the Queen displayed, and every Gĩkũyũ would be asked to take the oath of allegiance to the Queen and renounce the Mau Mau.

Each Gĩkũyũ should be photographed at the ceremony and issued with an armlet bearing the number of the photograph. Any Gĩkũyũ, without an armlet, would be suspect and liable to arrest.

With the support of the colonial authorities and the national traitors this anti-Mau Mau oath campaign was extended to Nairobi and Central Province.

Members of the Mau Mau movement, despite the brutal torture, refused to renounce the revolutionary struggle or to take the oath of allegiance to the British monarch; they preferred imprisonment or death. As a matter of fact, some of them were tortured to death, others were maimed for life, and many more were imprisoned without trial.

Letters to the Colonial Chiefs and Headmen

Land Freedom Army
HQ Nyandarwa
May 28, 1954

Dear Chief Kabucho,

Ndagũthaitha na nguo cia nyũkwa that you stop suppressing Mau Mau. If you continue I will have you eliminated. Also tell Chiefs Gĩcũhĩ, Gĩciriri, Samuel Wamũndũrũ, Lazaro Waicigo, Mbiro Mũgathĩ, Mwĩthuka Thaiya, Wanjohi Kĩmani, Mwangi Karogi, Gĩathirithi Gĩathĩ, Hosea Wainaina, Douglas Rĩgĩtarĩ, Mũrĩmi Njaũ, Mũciũĩ Kamau, Josphat Kamanda, Ngarĩ Gĩcamu, Mwaũra Kĩnyanjũi, William Gĩtũ, Daniel Karũithi, Dahara Karũho, Joshua Nyangũi and Head Richard Njoroge Njaũ that if they continue supporting the British occupiers in killing our people and destroying their property, I will order their extermination. They have probably forgotten the lesson of Lari.

I am sending this letter with the clear understanding that you will read it and take what I have said seriously. It really makes my blood boil to see our own people supporting the British who have occupied our country and reduced us to slavery.

We pay taxes, and yet we are not allowed to make decisions concerning policies for this country. How long shall we continue to pay a poll tax, and still continue to allow ourselves to be killed and our property to be confiscated?

We are fighting in order to liberate our people and our country. For those who stand in our way *'no kinya tũmonorie'*. We will crush them together with their families like we did in Lari.

Let me emphasize this: If you want me to come to Kĩambu, continue to suppress women and children. Don't you read newspapers to find out that we are winning this war? Can't you understand that your support of the British is a betrayal of your own people? Why do you want to die as a traitor?

In conclusion, let me say this: There is nothing which does not have its end. What I mean, in short, is that this war will end in our favour and, consequently, those who have betrayed our country and murdered our compatriots in support of the foreign occupiers will pay the ultimate price.

It is better to die for our country because the people will remember you forever.

F. M, Sir D. Kĩmathi

Dear Headman…

First accept my greetings, but, after this, listen carefully to what I am going to say. If you want to live, try and behave like Chief Mũhoya. I mean you should be neutral in this war. First of all, I don't want you to patrol at night because your men are harassing women and children; I have witnessed this several times when I passed through that area. However, despite your criminal act I have ordered my men not to eliminate you, but to seize your cattle as a form of punishment. But if you don't take this warning seriously, I will have no other choice but to cut you down.

I really pity all of you who are collaborating with the British—the enemy of our country. Being surrounded by trenches, daily parades and subjugated by rigid colonial orders, you suffer more than those of us who are championing the people's cause. But why suffer for crumbs? How terrible it is to die as a traitor.

I would like all of us, including you, to unite as a people in order to fight for our land and freedom. True, our sacrifice will be great and many of our compatriots will fall, but we will definitely win the war. And if we all die, the coming generation will pick up the revolutionary banner and continue the struggle.

This is all I wanted to tell you. Please, don't bother women and children any more.

Dedan Kĩmathi
Supreme Commander of the KLFA
Nyandarwa, 1954

Chief Kugudo Kavido,

Many greetings to you: to your father, mother, and children. I am appealing to you to assist all Gĩkũyũ who are forcibly brought there by the British authorities. Would you ask the other chiefs in the area to do the same?

I also want you to organize the Pokot youths in your area to join the Kenya Land and freedom Army in order to fight for land and freedom. Remember how [the British] mercilessly killed many Pokot youths, including our compatriot Lukas, during the Baringo confrontation. You are also aware that Europeans have taken our land, cattle, goats, and sheep. More and more are grabbed every month. This is clear proof that Europeans are our principal enemy.

As soon as the Pokot youths join the struggle against our common enemy, I will supply them with firearms. Once we free our motherland, the Pokot and other [nationalities] will have enough land to graze their livestock and to cultivate.

I think these few lines are enough. Your friends, Kagiri wa Ngumo and Mĩrigũ, send their regards. Kagiri is planning to visit you to the near future. He is now a great Captain in our liberation army.

Yours,
Dedan Kĩmathi
May 23, 1954

Dear Chief Philip Kioko,

This is to inform you that I have dispatched General Vido to that region with an army of 1500 strong. He is in the Yatta area at the moment. If you want to save your life, you should be careful how you treat General Vido and his army. My advice is that you should take a neutral stand in this war, as Chief Mūhoya has done, otherwise General Vido will not hesitate to cut off your head.

The British are the enemy of our people and it is about time that we Africans united against these foreign robbers. Remember that many Wakamba youths were slaughtered during the two World Wars fighting for the British; but what did the Wakamba get for their bravery and loyalty? Their reward was to have their cattle, goats and sheep confiscated for the benefit of the white settlers.

For this reason, I am asking you not to be taken in by British propaganda. Mau Mau is the cry of a people suffering from poverty and exploitation. It is a vehicle to liberate our country—to regain the Kenyan soil which the Europeans have occupied by force. You should encourage the Wakamba youths to join Mau Mau; this will strengthen our position and, above all, help us to dislodge these foreign robbers from our land.

If war is bad Europeans would not have been fighting. In other words, war for the liberation of one's country is a just war.

Marshal D. Kĩmathi

Letters to Tanganyika

P.O. Box 102
Arusha, Tanganyika

Dear Mr. Sylvanus Kaaya,

This is a fair warning to you not to harass the Gĩkũyũ who are in that area. The Gĩkũyũ are good people who are being oppressed by Europeans; a people whose land, cattle and other wealth have been forcibly confiscated.

You are not such a fool as to ignore the fact that your people have also been oppressed by white settlers. You are a great chief; it is therefore your duty to think about your people first. Let our two peoples unite and fight against this [colonial] slavery.

The land which the white settlers have occupied here in Kenya is ours; our intention is hence to unite all of our people, and to fight until this land is returned to us. For this reason, do not treat the Gĩkũyũ as your enemies, but as your friends. I once tried to set up a political organization on behalf of the Wameru in Tanganyika, but the forces of imperialism cut me off.

In conclusion, think about your country and the freedom of the African. Do not be deceived by the money or sweet words from these White robbers; they are nothing but blood-suckers.

I am the Commander-in-Chief of all Kenya Armies.

Marshal D. Kĩmathi

P.O. Box Tanga
Tanganyika

Dear Mr. Salehe Kibwana,

I hope you are well. I understand that you are collaborating with the Kenya settlers to harass and arrest the Gĩkũyũ for being members of Mau Mau.

I would like to inform you that what is being referred to as Mau Mau is a genuine struggle of African people against British slavery. As an African, therefore, you should not support the British against the Gĩkũyũ. Don't you believe in the struggle for land and freedom?

It is not true that we are against civilization, that our aims are to take our people back to ancient times. Our fighting is for the return of our stolen land and freedom. If you can remember, the Europeans have occupied our best land and have also reduced us to slavery.

We are not savages or murderers as the British continue to claim. We know what we are doing; and we know what is best for our people.

It is in this connection that I ask you not to be blinded by British lies, propaganda or money. I think you, and Mr. Mohammed Ali and Mr. M.M. Kihere are the patriotic leaders of the African people. You are the only leaders who can organize the people to fight for land and freedom in that region, but it is better to know that freedom does not come through love, but through fierce struggle. In short, the journey to freedom is full of sacrifices—tears, hunger, clothes full of lice, blood and death.

Imagine the thousands of Africans who lost their lives during the two World Wars. What did they die for, and did we benefit from these wars? Our reward was slavery.

Furthermore, it is important to understand that all this love that the British preach is nothing but a cover for our exploitation. In reality, the British colonialists hate us and wish us death. For that reason, I urge you to unite with us to fight our freedom. Let us offer our own lives for the freedom of our people. If we sacrifice our lives for our country, our people will never forget us; they will immortalize our names.

On my part, I consider myself a great African patriot fighting, not for the liberation of Kenya alone, but for East Africa and the rest of the continent. I believe that the liberation of [Nigeria or] any other African country will strengthen our liberation [struggle].

Field Marshal D. Kĩmathi

P.O. Box Tanga
May 23, 1954
Tanganyika

Dear Olkarsia Safania Smeli,

I am writing to request that you not cooperate with the Europeans who are mistreating the Gĩkũyũ, for the Gĩkũyũ are fighting for the liberation of the Kenyan people. Mau Mau is, therefore, the backbone of that struggle.

We would also like you to know that we are not only fighting for the liberation of Kenya, but of East Africa as a whole. In this regard, your support will strengthen our force.

With these few lines, I am asking you to treat the Gĩkũyũ people as freedom fighters—support them against the common enemy.

It is better to die than to live in misery and slavery.

Marshal D. Kĩmathi
The Leader of the War in Kenya

Terms for Negotiation

General China to Kĩmathi

General China W. I.
February 16, 1954

Dear D. Kĩmathi,
Greetings as usual.

I am writing to tell you about the development of the situation since I was captured. As you have already heard, I was shot by the enemy in the battle on January 15, 1954, and captured. The bullet passed through the veins on my neck; even my throat was seriously injured. I could hardly breathe.

On February 3, 1954, I was sentenced to death by the [British] court at Nyeri. I have appealed against my sentence but I don't know whether they will accept my appeal. However, whatever they decide does not matter much to me. At any rate, as soon as I hear from you I will let you know their final decision.

I have had several talks with [colonial] government officials, and I have given them a letter to send to the governor. During our discussions, they asked me why you lead terrorists, and what prevents them from surrendering. I told them that they don't surrender because they fear being killed. In this regard, I tried to enlighten them on the mistakes they make when they capture the freedom fighters, particularly the guerrilla leaders, and kill them instead of talking to them in order to know the reason behind the fighting and how it can be stopped. Furthermore, I told them that if they want guerrillas to surrender, they should remove their armed forces from the 'reserve' as a gesture of good will or compromise. But there are some questions they asked me concerning this issue. That is, if they remove their armed forces from the 'reserve', what will happen to the *'thata cia bũrũri'*? What will happen to those who collaborated with [colonial] government? I told them that I could not give them definite answers to these questions until I had consulted you.

In the meantime, I agreed with the British officials that it was possible to arrange a conference in order to discuss our surrender. We agreed that four guerrilla leaders (two from Nyandarwa and two from Kĩrĩnyaga) should attend the conference. The British Government sends its own four representatives; two will be appointed by the Governor; General Erskine will appoint the other two. They have assured me that if guerrilla leaders attend the conference they will not be harmed or arrested, and that they will be allowed to return to the forest to report the proceedings of the conference, but they have made it clear that I will not be released until all of you have come out of the forest.

In connection with this, they [the British Government] would like to know your position on the following questions:

1. Are you willing to accept a ceasefire so that the negotiations to end the war can start?
2. Do you think it is appropriate to send four guerrilla leaders to attend the surrender conference?
3. In regard to the fact that the [British Government] is calling for a peace conference, do you think it is trying to trick us?
4. What are your terms for negotiation?

In conclusion, I want you to understand the reality of the situation and to realize that I am talking to you as one of the guerrilla leaders. Therefore, I am insisting that we agree to attend the surrender conference. One thing is certain: if the negotiations fail to take place, if we refuse to surrender, the British are determined to continue fighting. My views are that if we don't negotiate for surrender now, there will not be any other chance. Remember, we are fighting both Europeans and Africans.

Please give me your views regarding these important issues. You can contact me through the following address:

W. I. Kīmani
P.O. Box 21
Naro Maro

I use this address so that the Europeans on the farms will not confiscate the letter. You know they don't want such things.

Goodbye.
Yours,
General China

Kīmathi's Reply to General China's Letter

Editor's note: The letter was sent directly to the British [colonial] authorities; it states:

These are the answers to your questions:

1. If the [British forces] withdraw from the countryside, we will not kill the *'thata cia būrūri'*. The basic reason if that we know many of them are victims of British propaganda. Generally, we believe in reconciliation and harmony between races.

2. Many Africans, including those who are helping the [British] Government in this war, generally long to see peace restored in the country. We believe that the unconditional withdrawal of your armed forces from the country, particularly from the African Reserves, will restore peace in the nation and cooperation among the people.

3. Those of other races—especially Indians and Arabs—who have sided with your government in this war will have to leave the country, [together with White settlers], when we regain our self-government. The rest have nothing to fear; they are welcome to stay.

4. I don't lead terrorists; I lead Africans who want their self-government and land. I lead them because God never created any nation to be ruled

by another nation forever. Furthermore, we cannot allow anybody to deprive our [birthright]. If anyone wants to take our [birthright] away, he has first to kill all of us. Terrorists are persons who commit evil deeds, while we do the opposite. Of course, the [colonial] government is practicing terrorism and continuing to commit barbaric acts against our people, hence it has no right whatsoever to call us terrorists.

5. The call for peace negotiations is a dirty trick to kill my guerrilla soldiers. We cannot forget that after our gentlemanly agreement of August 8, 1953 that both sides should observe a ceasefire while peace negotiations were going on, your government took advantage of this-- arrested and murdered several of my best men.

6. My soldiers will never leave these forests until the British Government accepts our demands:

    a) disarm its forces unconditionally;
    b) release all the political prisoners; and
    c) recognize our country's independence.

These are our terms for negotiation.
Field Marshal D. Kĩmathi
Ref: EFI/3/3/620

Release the KAU Leaders

Editor's Note: On April 3, 1954, Kĩmathi issued another statement concerning the peace negotiations. Copies of this statement were sent to Governor Baring, General Erskine, the British Prime Minister, Clement Attlee, and the President of the Soviet Union. Several copies of this statement were circulated in Nairobi and were published by different newspapers in the city. The Citizen, a Nairobi weekly newspaper, was one of them. The statement was signed by Kĩmathi's private secretary; it reads:

1. If the ceasefire is to be arranged with immediate effect, our people are *only* ready to listen to the African leaders now in detention, it is only

the release of those leaders that would convince [us] and the world the [British] Government really wants peace.

2. It is useless to expect the African members of the Legislative Council to conduct such negotiations. It must be borne in mind that up to now they are not our chosen representatives; they are [colonial] Government African nominated members. How can you expect us to have confidence in them? When matters come to a head, they have no public to turn to for a vote of confidence.

3. General China is a sensible man, but we must state in no uncertain terms that we will not be moved by his pleas, unless he and the [British] Government agree to the *Charter* issued last year by F.M. Dedan Kĩmathi.

4. China is one of the qualified Generals in Kenya. We therefore thank the Governor of Kenya, Sir Baring, and General Erskine for the thoughtful way in which they have treated our honored General. But we stress that it is absolute nonsense to reorganize the Government of Kenya today without first acting upon the points raised in the *Charter.*

5. We are not fighting for an everlasting hatred, but we are trying to create a true and real brotherhood between White and Black, so that we may be regarded as people, as human beings, who can do each and everything [once they are free and independent.]

6. No green branches will be raised in Kenya. In other words, there will be no ceasefire until our demands are met.

I remeber my hurt, my anguish, my indignation, my painful tears snaking dowm my facing, when Kimathi was shot and captured. The whole of my world collapsed. To us Kimathi symbolized our indestructible vitality and of that strength which the Kenyan people managed to concretize together in their efforts to drive the British imperialist occupiers out of our homeland. He will always be a part of the soil of Kenya.

Interview, Njoki wa Ndùng'ù, Nakuru, 1976

Jomo Kenyatta (2nd in line) was arrested on October 20, 1952, falsely accused of being the leader of the Mau Mau movement, and imprisoned to seven years of hard labor.

Statue of Dedan Kĩmathi in Nairobi.

The Mau Mau Monuments at Uhuru, Park Nairobi. Courtesy of Heavyconscious Movement.

Mau Mau Made Guns

With these guns and the massive support of the Kenyan people, the Kenya Land and Freedom Army (KLFA) took on the mighty army of the British Empire. The end of the Mau Mau War was also the end of the British Empire in Kenya and the rest of Africa.

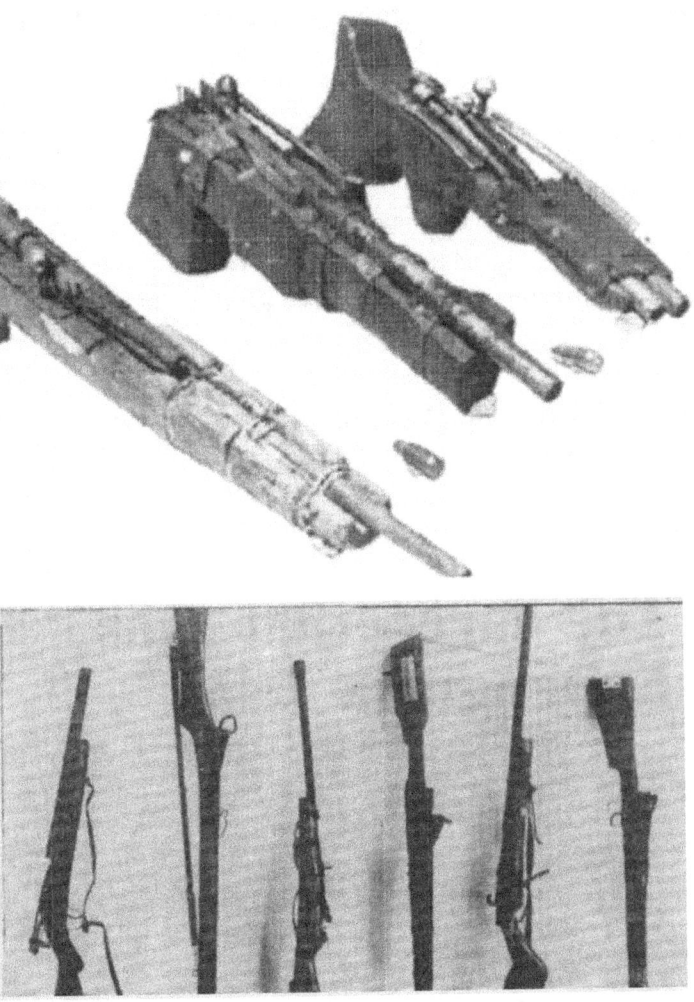

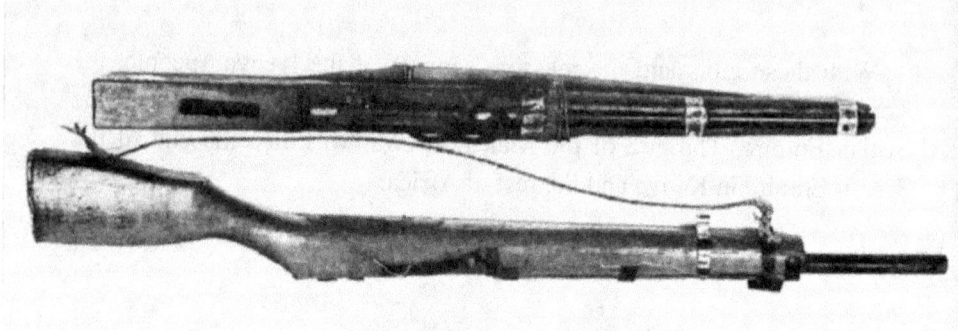

These guns identify us, they define us; they tell the story of who we are as Kenyans. But it is also a powerful story of people – of courageous, dauntless and patriotic people who made great sacrifice for the liberation of their country from imperialist occupation. Hence, it is impossible not to admire Dedan Kĩmathi and his comrades-in-arms for their revolutionary firmness and the strength of their argument and conviction.

PART 4
Firmly Demand the Total Withdrawal of British Forces from Our Country

Letters to the Kenya Parliament

The Liquidationists Must Be Fought

To the Kenya Parliament

Just a brief note to inform you about what is happening with us down here; we are working day and night for our people and country.

According to our intelligence task force, there are liquidationists bent on seizing our armed organization and eliminating our genuine patriots. On January 1, 1954, for instance, General Kahiũ-Itina and Kĩbirũ attacked me and seized my gun after a struggle. They are using false accusations to justify their actions against the people. They said that I didn't lead my force well, implying that my force didn't fight the enemy as it was supposed to. They said that they wanted to reorganize the entire guerrilla army. The same day they attacked Kĩnyua wa Wawerũ and Thũre wa Gĩtonga and took their guns.

Two weeks later, on January 13th, General Kahiũ-Itina returned and showed me a letter which stated that the Marshal would be relieved of his responsibilities because of his political impotency and that he loved women too much, contrary to the rules and regulations of the movement. The letter went on to say that if we allowed the Marshal to continue with his undignified behavior, he would turn the majority of the guerrilla women into prostitutes. He wanted me and my force to support him and his group, but I adamantly refused. I told him to bring this matter before the Parliament, but he rejected my suggestion.

Since this is a very serious matter, the KLFA Supreme Commander should take a strong stand against these renegades. Our fighting tradition dictates that we mercilessly wipe them out.

Yours comradely,
Commander Rũanjane

A Warning Circular

To the Kenya Parliament

There is an unconfirmed report that the enemy is organizing a major attack on us—ground and air forces will be used during the attack. It is likely that the enemy offensive will start on May 4, 1954, but this is not definite.

My advice, therefore, is that our forces should take precautions and be ready to punish these killers of innocent people.

Similarly, it has been confirmed that the British are bringing in 2,000 more soldiers in their effort to strengthen their shaky forces in the country. The soldiers will be arriving here in May. With the bringing of these thousands of soldiers, it is definitely true that the British authorities are contemplating genocide against our people.

However, I am certain that the strength of our struggle will force the British to accept our demands: land and freedom.

This is all I wanted you to know.
May Ngai (God) be with you always.

Your comrade,
Colonel Wamũgũnda
April 25, 1954

The Kinangop-Kĩnyũmi Army Unit

To the Kenya Parliament

This is to inform you that the troops in the Kinangop-Kĩnyũmi region are under General Mũraya wa Mbuthia, and that these are their difficulties:

1. Lack of clothes and medicine: **a)** right now there are more than 15 comrades with bullet wounds, but there is no medicine to treat them; and, **b)** several comrades are in rags. They particularly need heavy coats for this place is extremely cold.
2. Our greatest complaint is that things which are sent through the Mũrang'a Front do not reach us. We would like the Parliament to investigate this issue.

KLFA Battalions and their Commanders

To the K.P. Members

This is the report you had asked me to circulate. I apologize that it could not reach you earlier than this.

1. Ituma Ndemi Battalion:
    No. 1: General Kahiũ-Itina
    No. 2: General Kitura
2. Gĩkũyũ Iregi Battalion:
    No. 1: General Kago
    No. 2: General Ihũũra
    No. 3: Brigadier Njatũ
3. MEI Mathathi Battalion:
    No. 1: General Tanganyika
    No. 2: General Achira
    No. 3: General Kubukubu
    No. 4: General Bamũinge
    No. 5: General Mwariama
4. Kenya Levellation Battalion:
    No.1: General Kariba
    No. 2: general Kamami
    No. 3: General Mũkũra
5. Townwatch Battalion:
    No. 1: General Enoch Mwangi
6. Highlands (Mbũrũ) Ngebo Battalion:

No. 1: General Gacerū
No. 2: General Kīmbo,
No. 3: General Mūraya

This last battalion includes all settled areas from Nanyuki, Nyahururu, Nakuru to Kapenguria. Everyone who came from Rift Valley before or after the outbreak of the present struggle for land and freedom must be associated with this battalion. All officers and other ranks will, in the future, be known by the name of their battalion.

Decentralization of the KLFA Forces

To the Parliament

I hereby notify you that the undermentioned comrades have been appointed to lead the units within the Ituma Ndemi Army (INA). These arrangements are in accordance with the recent decision of the Kenya Parliament to decentralize the KLFA forces.

1st. INA Commander:	General Ndīritū Thūita
2nd. INA Commander:	General Kīhara Kagumu
3rd. INA Commander:	Karari Njama
4th. INA Commander:	General Kahinga Wachanga
5th. INA Commander:	General Gīkonyo wa Kanyūngū
6th. INA Commander:	Major General Ndūrūri wa Gītitika
7th. INA Commander:	General Gitonga wa Mūthūi
Divisional Commander:	Kabūga Njogu

I hope the Parliament will accept these new arrangements. As soon as the Parliament approves these appointments, the Secretary-General should stamp the letter officially and circulate it among the fighting forces immediately.

I am disappointed that I don't get answers to my letters, nor do you send me newspapers. I am really puzzled about this silence.

F. Marshal D. Kĩmathi

Recommendation for joining the Guerrilla Army

To the Kenya Parliament

Hannah Wamũyũ is an educated and intelligent girl; she loves her country and people very much. Although many educated women cannot be trusted nowadays, Wamũyũ can be. She is a committed and a serious patriot.

She is a trained nurse; so she can help in reorganizing our hospitals. She can also type.

I am, therefore, recommending that she should be allowed to join the liberation army.

Marshal D. Kĩmathi

Kĩmathi to Guerrillas

Ref. No. EFI/3/3/529
Kenya Land and Freedom Army
HQ Nyandarwa
March 2, 1954

Dear General Kago,
Many greetings.

First I want to inform you that I am proud of your courage and patriotism. If we have many leaders like you we will be able to develop our guerrilla army into an invincible force. There is no doubt – your steely leadership and revolutionary commitment are a great example to all of us.

The report you sent to the Kenya Parliament is encouraging. I strongly believe that through your leadership and commitment, we will be able to liberate Mũrang'a district before the end of this year. General Kariba has also forced the enemy to evacuate a large area of Nyeri district, and, according to his recent report, his strategy is to liberate the whole region by the end of the year.

From your report we also learnt about the atrocities and brutalities that the British forces are committing against our people – solely because they dared demand their human rights and the land which was stolen from them. The British talk of 'democracy', but is it democracy when hundreds of our people are sent to the cemetery for saying that they want our independence and our land back? Perhaps the British don't understand the meaning of our struggle; we have repeatedly said that we will fight until we drive them out of this land – we shall never surrender.

Did you receive the circular I sent to all Front Commanders concerning General China's surrender? China has agreed to collaborate with our enemy, to work against the homeland, to save his neck. In this connection, he has told the enemy all he knows about the movement, including our military secrets. Furthermore, in order to prove his loyalty to his new friends, he has written to all [Kĩrĩnyaga] Front Commanders and the members of the Kenya parliament urging them to call off the fighting and surrender to the British forces. I received a copy of his letter and when I read it, I was filled with indignation. If China thinks I will mortgage this great struggle to save his life, he must be crazy!

We have written to China and denounced him for his treacherous acts. We have, at the same time, made it clear to the British authorities that we will not lay down our arms until they dismantle their war machine and leave the country.

In these circumstances, my advice is simply this: you should have a general meeting with our forces and try to explain our position to them. Tell them to be more valiant and ruthless against the British effort to sell their terms of surrender to our people. During the meeting, stress the importance of unity and national patriotism and denounce China's treacherous acts simultaneously.

Be satisfied with these few lines for now. I will let you know when and where the next KLFA General Conference will be held.

Marshal Dedan Kĩmathi

Editor's note: General Kago was known for his aggressively and ruthlessly strategy, but also for his superhuman courage and uncompromised stand. He embodied Kenya's revolution and dignity and its fight against the British imperialist occupiers. His spirit and soul live on in each of our hearts.

Dear General Ihũũra,

I received your report and I was happy to learn about the progress of the war on that front. The best thing to do, if the enemy intensified its bombing, is to divide the army into small units which will be easier to scatter when the attacks come. Large camps are also dangerous because they can be surrounded easily.

I have sent the things you wanted and one copy of your report for your file. Tell our warriors to fight with determination; there is no doubt that we will win this war no matter how long it will take.

A report I received recently informs me that the Kenya Liberation Army Unit, under Brigadier Nduati and Colonel Manyeki Wang'ombe, is doing an excellent job in Kĩharũ Division. When you contact them, let them know that the Kenya Parliament is proud of their revolutionary work.

F.M. Dedan Kĩmathi
HQ Nyandarwa

EFI/3/3/528
April 1954

Dear Major Kĩng'ori,

I am writing to ask you and young comrades not to be disheartened by the loss inflicted upon you by the enemy. Tell your men to have courage; tell them to remember that even if we die, this war will continue and our land will one day be free.

When I received news of the battle, I was not happy to hear that we had lost quite a number of our compatriots. However, you should know that bad luck sometimes falls on people and such losses do occur. But in spite of all this, we have made a pledge to our people never to leave these forests until our country is free. So when death occurs it should be taken as one step forward towards our goal.

Finally, I would like you to know that I received a letter from Mr. Fenner Brockway and another one from Mbiyũ wa Koinange. Both letters support our struggle and provide us with great encouragement.

D Kĩmathi

Fenner Brockway's reply states:

Dear Kamau (using a code name to hide identity),

I am in receipt of your letter. I read it with great sympathy. I have handed over the letter to Ralph Milner and Johnson who will deal with the affairs in Parliament.

Yours faithfully,
Fenner Brockway

May 5, 1954

Dear Colonel Wamũgũnda,

I have received many of your letters concerning the British policy of land consolidation. I want to make it clear that no one should accept the consolidation of his land or support this evil policy; you should not hesitate to cut him down. This is an order.

We are also not going to buy the land which was stolen from us. It is a crime for any of us to discuss the land question when we are still fighting for it.

We received the following items:

1. 2 pairs of trousers
2. 2 tents
3. 10 sock
4. 27 tablets of tapeworm medicine

The money has not arrived and we have not yet received the bars of soap.

The enclosed letter belongs to Muturi 5/5. Please give it to him. There is a woman I would like to meet. She stays at Nyangarithi, near the pig camp beyond Rūrūngū. Her name is Miriamu Wanjirū wa Ndegwa. Tell your wife to fetch her and take her to Lea's house. I will meet her there. In the meantime, these are the directives I would like your wife to follow: when she arrives at Thūita's place, she must leave the road which goes to Gīakanja towards Nderi's homeguard camp, and follow the one which goes to Gacatha. When she passes the pig's camp, she will see Mariamu's place; if she does not see the house she can ask where it is. Once she finds Mariamu, she should tell her that I want to see her.

The woman is one of the prominent leaders of our struggle. I once worked with her in the Rift Valley before the start of our armed struggle, where she was responsible for politicizing the masses. She was carrying the struggle to every big town.

I would like her to come to the forest for two weeks for a serious discussion. I want her to start organizing our women in her village.

In the meantime, I would like to have some new trousers; I gave the ones you sent me to a guerrilla who needed them more than I did. If you are buying cordoury, please get one yard for 15 shillings. It is better to spend 100 shillings on good trousers than to buy one which cannot last even for one month.

I have not yet received the money orders which I asked for. I have enclosed 50 shillings to buy me a money order. I would like to send it to India; so send it immediately.

Ask Karūmaindo whether he has received any magazines and newspapers from Nairobi. Also tell him to send the books he promised me. You should also tell him to stop opening my letters.

I have informed our guerrillas that you are in charge of that region and I have told them that they should consult you if they are in the area. I think they are aware of this now.

Finally, I would like to inform you that I have sent a letter to several individuals in England concerning the justness of our struggle.

In conclusion, please forward the money order as soon as you receive this letter.

Matemo [Marshal D.K.]

Dear Colonel Wamũgũnda,
Greetings as usual.

In recognition of the good of his revolutionary work, I have promoted Comrade Thiga to the rank of Corporal, with effect from May 24, 1954. Though Comrade Thiga is very young (not yet 19 years of age), his dedication to the liberation of our people is well known to all of us. It is true that '*Njamba ti ikere*' [Hero's strength does not dwell in one's appearance, but rather in the mind, intellect, convictions, commitment and virtue].

You should work closely with him, advice him about all aspects of his work. Give him the enclosed 5 shillings on behalf of the Government of Gĩkũyũ and Mũmbi.

Marshal D. K.

May 24, 1954

Dear Colonel Wamũgũnda,

I do not have flour, sugar, or maize. However, so long as Wamanga is leading her group, their work should continue even at night. She is the only woman you can rely on in that area.

Wanjũki has given orders that the books and letter in your possession, and the ones in Ihũrũrũ, should be hidden because the enemy is planning a search in the area.

It is better to die than to surrender.

D.K.

May 20, 1954

Army Commander Magũ,

I was both surprised and delighted by the letter I received from your yesterday. I would say that *'Mwana wĩna mũreri ndarĩaga mai'* or *' Irĩ kuuma kĩmamo ndĩcokaga'*. Let us work hard for the liberation of our people. In working for our people, we are doing God's work.

I have been informed that reading my letters is prohibited in the great city of Nairobi. If one is caught doing so, he will be severely punished. I have also heard that after reading the letter I sent them, the Russian Government has decided to lock up the British Foreign Minister. Mau Mau has become part and parcel of the struggle against imperialism in the world. I also read that they are showing a film about our struggle entitled 'Simba'.

You should wait for us on the night of May 25, 1954, or on May 26, 1954; we are not sure whether Major Vido will be ready by May 25th. He is the only one who may delay us.

We are desperately in need of ammunition, particularly for the .303 rifles. Try to get some for us. Also tell Major Jeriko to provide us with grenades. I understand he has more than five.

As far as security preparations are concerned, order Colonel Totha and Commander Kĩng'ori to destroy the bridges at Bama School and Kĩnainĩ before our arrival. The Kĩnainĩ bridge will be little harder to destroy because it is made of stone, but it must be destroyed. Both bridges must be destroyed tonight. The job will be easier if the Ituma and Kĩmũrĩ Units get together to discharge this important task.

See to it that there is strict discipline when the task is carried out. In this regard, only those who have been hardened by the struggle should be assigned this task.

Marshal D. Kĩmathi

Dear Colonel Wambararia,

How are things over there? I have received several reports from our front commanders, who are concerned about the progress of our struggle, and I am proud to say that despite his sophisticated weaponry and the support he has received from his Kenyan allies, the enemy has failed to halt our offensive. There is no doubt that the enemy forces are exhausted; I think this is one of the reasons why both Governor Baring and General Erskine have constantly been urging me to attend peace negotiations. But I have consistently told the British rulers that there will be no peace talks until they accept the following demands:

1. Disarm their force.
2. Release all political prisoners.
3. Recognize our country's national independence.

We will never negotiate with them until they unconditionally accept these three demands. They should know that we are not ready to sell our country for crumbs.

Recently, I have been dreaming constantly—mainly about our struggle. The other day, for instance, I dreamt that we had won the war and we marched to Nairobi with guns on hands, where we were given a tumultuous welcome by the people. On the following day, I declared our country free and ordered the arrest of the British Governor and those Kenyans who had helped him murder our compatriots. But I woke up before I had the chance to order their execution.

Last night I, again, dreamt that I was talking with our God about the struggle. It was a fantastic dream. I felt someone take hold of my hand in my sleep, I woke up and heard *Mwene-Nyaga* saying to me: "My son, come with me". I stood up and followed Him. We walked together, discussing our glorious struggle. We passed through a very beautiful forest where there were many red and yellow flowers and hostile birds with red wings. When there, these birds saw us, and they started exclaiming: "Kĩmathi, we are with you! Do not give up the struggle!" There were many big shining rocks around us, and clean springs were flowing from them. Across the valley, there were thousands of women from all Kenyan [nationalities] singing songs of praise of our heroic struggle. I was really moved. We walked to a *Mũgumo* tree, which was bigger and taller than all other trees in the forest—a tree that was like the king of all trees. I rested my hand upon it, then *Ngai* spoke to me again: "Kĩmathi," he said calmly, "this is my dwelling place and here I will guide and protect you. I will make sure that your enemy is defeated and that peace will return to this beautiful land." Then, suddenly, the tree came up out of the ground and ascended up into the clouds and disappeared. It rained very heavily after that. The morning call for breakfast interrupted my dream and I woke up.

This is just one of my dreams. What do you make of it?

Have you heard from home? I understand that they have arrested our mother and taken her to the Kamĩtĩ detention camp. Since Mũkami [Kĩmathi's wife] is already there, she will take care of her. Besides, she is a courageous woman; she will fight her way through. I was also informed that they confiscated our *shamba* [land] and gave it to the homeguards. There is no question that the detention of my wife, my mother, the confiscation of our land, and the harassment of relatives and in-laws is a desperate attempt to force me to surrender. But you know my stance. I would rather die than betray our people's struggle.

I would like to write you a long letter, but I have to prepare for a session of the Kenya Parliament. So let these few lines be enough for now.

Greet all our comrades. Tell them to fight with vigour and determination. There is no doubt that we will win this war.

Marshal D. K.

May 24, 1954

Dear Colonel Wambararia,
Many greetings.

We should meet before May 30, 1954. Please inform Major Thia, Captain Baragũ and Lieutenant Gateru about this. I have talked to Commander Ndĩritũ wa Thũita, Nyaga, Abdullah and a few other comrades, and they have agreed that we should get together to review our situation.

Mwangi has also told me that there is a group within the movement which is plotting to kill you, Thũnjira, Ndĩritũ wa Thũita and myself. In a situation as serious as this, we should unite all our forces and prepare for a bloody confrontation with these liquidationist elements.

Has your illness been cured? I gave Captain Baragũ 30 shillings and a pair of shoes to bring to you. Did you receive them? I also gave Captain Baragũ 30 shillings for himself.

I received a letter from Kanyinga the other day. He tells me that your men went to Karũnainĩ and took a woman by force and brought her to the forest. Order these comrades to return that woman to her home. Our rules are clear: it is a serious crime to force individuals to join the guerrilla army without their consent.

I am planning to go to Chania and I would like you to join me there. Tell Lieutenant Gateru to inform the four guerrilla women, from Kanjora, to be present when we arrive there. On their arrival, they should go to the house of Joyce, the wife of Gĩkonyo wa Mahinda, who will direct them to Leah Wambũi wa Mũtunga's house. Under no circumstances should they fail to come. I want to assign them a very important task.

Marshal D. Kĩmathi

May 24, 1954

Major Thia,

We are alright here. *Ngai* willing, I shall arrive there on May 26, 1954. I think you, Mūrūa-mbararia, Ndīritū wa Thūita and I should get together to discuss the war situation: how to get more guns, and how to attack the enemy forces, particularly the *thata cia būrūri* (the barren of the country). Find out whether it is possible to attack the Kanyinga homeguard post.

We will surely win this struggle if we stand firm and united. Our problem is now those renegades within the armed movement who are determined to undermine the struggle by killing some of us.

You should begin to get ready to go to Chania for the KLFA General Conference on May 31, 1954. I think the new woman comrade in your unit should go to the village and inform the village KLFA leaders about this important conference which they should also attend. She knows the way to Chania.

Although the other women guerrillas are trying to resent her leadership, because she is a new cadre; I think that she is more politically advanced and daring than most of them. If she does not want to go for security reasons, don't send any other woman on this mission.

That is all.

Marshal D. Kīmathi

May 28, 1954

Dear Comrade Maribu,

You are invited, together with other members of the KLFA Village Committee, to attend the 'Heroes' Day celebrations, which will take place here in Nyandarwa on June 6, 1954. All our supporters—men, women and children – are also invited.

In order to make this day a success, I am asking the following members of the movement to help us with the following items:

1. Macarubu: to provide 10 loaves of bread;
2. Waithaka wa Kĩbutu: to provide 2 tins of coffee and 5 lbs of sugar;
3. Kĩhara wa Gakuo: to provide 2 bags of white flour and 2 tins of coffee
4. Gaciri wa Mũita: to provide 5 lbs of cooking oil;
5. Mũhoro wa Gĩtonga: to provide 3 bottles of milk;
6. Gĩtahi wa Gacoka: 5 lbs of sugar;
7. Ndũng'ũ wa Gathuma: 5 tins of coffee; and
8. Karagũ: 5 lbs of sugar.

These things will be collected on May 31, 1954.

We are also asking the women to bring supplies of potatoes, yams, maize, flour, beans and bananas. The girls are required to provide handkerchiefs to wipe off perspiration and threads and buttons. We are also asking Waithaka wa Mũraya, Gĩtonya wa ihũre, and all the elders to provide *njohi* (beer) for the ceremony. All these things will be collected on June 5th, by Comrade Wanjũki, the compatriots who sell snuff.

Make sure that you contact these compatriots before the deadline; explain to each and every one what they are supposed to do. Tell them that this is an order. If you fail to contact them, you will have committed a serious crime for which you will be held responsible.

Marshal D. Kĩmathi

Dear Maingĩ wa Thũita,

Greetings.

You will assume, with immediate effect, the post of a headman and KLFA Village Committee leader. Make sure that you do not sell the community for money. Any attempt, or even the thought, of betraying the people is an unforgiveable crime. Your main task will be as follows:

1. To protect young boys from being killed or used as spies by our enemy.
2. To help women whose husbands are in the forest, have been detained, or have been killed by the enemy.
3. To collect clothing and food for guerrilla fighters.
4. To collect KLFA subscriptions from the people: men should pay 62/50 shillings, young women: 12/50 shillings, married women: 11/50 shillings, and young girls and boys over 15 years old: 2 shillings.
5. To organize the village against our enemy and opportunists.

That is all.

Marshal D. Kĩmathi
Nyandarwa HQ

Dear Bwana Muturi 5/5,
Many greetings.

Why don't you reply to my letters? Does this mean you don't want to work for our country? If you have agreed to work for our people, as Colonel Wamũgũnda has told me, I would advise you to forward your full name, the name of your clan, location, division and district. This information must reach the Kenya Parliament in Nairobi before you start working for the movement.

Since Colonel Wamũgũnda has recommended you highly in terms of your commitment and dedication, I will attach you to him. In fact, I have already told him to work closely with you and to assist you in all your [revolutionary] endeavors. The cadres who will be under your leadership must be well-guided politically, hardened enough to be able to defend the struggle from being destroyed. Apart from that, your primary duty is to protect and defend Gĩkũyũ and Mũmbi—men, women and children—from the enemy's attacks. The loss of one of them is a great loss to our country.

It is also your duty to see that the rules and regulations of the movement are followed. Furthermore, it is your responsibility to supply the guerrilla army with war materials and with information concerning the enemy's war efforts.

Work very hard for the people; work without the fear of death for we will all die one day. Besides, to die for one's country is to live forever.

To conclude, I'm looking forward to your support, after which I shall render you my services.

Supreme Commander of the Kenya Army

Chief of Staff Major Vido,

I am not happy because I haven't heard a word from you in the last few days. The war situation on our side is not bad, but my worry is that there are some units which have run out of food and clothing. My suggestion, therefore, is that we should try to help each other by sharing what we have. I have sent some field secretaries to see that this is accomplished before July 18, 1954.

Right now, the important thing is to get together and re-examine our war strategy. I feel that we should intensify our propaganda in the whole country and the world in general. In this connection our propaganda should be concentrated more on the Kenyan youths and school children. By doing so, we will form an invincible national army. In the meantime, try to see me so that we can arrange everything.

Marshal D. Kĩmathi

Land Freedom Army
Nyandarwa HQ

Dear 122 Kahiũkogĩ,

Greetings.

I was informed by Kamakoloni that you are working hard on the assignment given to you by the Kenya Parliament. I told him to tell you that you should put all your efforts into it because this work is very significant for the future generations. It should be done with care and dedication. Meanwhile, I would like to have the names of all the comrades you are working with. Also send me the names of their locations, clans and sub-locations for our records.

To come back to the subject of my letter, the work you are doing is significant because it will help the future Kenyan historians understand the heroism of the Mau Mau movement. Our activities, therefore, should be examined, documented and arranged as follows:

1. List all the names of those compatriots—men, women and children—who have been murdered by the enemy since the beginning of the war. Their locations, clans and sub-locations should also be listed.
2. List the names of our detained compatriots, their locations, clans and sub-locations.
3. Record the names of the partisans who are supporting the struggle in your region.
4. List the names, including their locations, sub-locations and clans of those who have sided with the enemy against our people.

Make sure that everyone who has taken part, for and against, in this struggle is included in this historical document. As soon as you have documented everything send the books to me for vetting. This should be done every month.

We need books, pens and pencils. Please send them to us, together with anything else you think can help us up here.

I am looking forward to your reply.

Field Marshal D. Kĩmathi

Dear Colonel Wamũgũnda,

Greetings.

Try to put every effort in organizing food for the guerrillas. We need plenty of ammunition because I don't want to see the guerrillas walking with empty rifles. The cadre who goes to Nyeri town for ammunition should go more regularly...send me the following books:

1. Napolean *Book of* fate: shs. 7.75
2. Zadkiel's *Book of Dreams:*   shs. 7.75
3. *Universal Dream Book*   shs. 4.75
4. *Tricks with Cards*   shs. 3.75
5. *Fortune Teller Book*   shs. 5.00
6. *Complete Letter writer:*   shs. 7.75
7. *How to Live 100 years:*   shs. 6.75
8. *Carbon paper:*   shs. <u>3.75</u>
   Total   shs. <u>47.25</u>

Other things I want are:

1. Corduroy trousers, size 30 x 44 x 17:   shs. 35.00
2. Corduroy trousers, size 29 x 47 x 17:   shs. 35.00
3. File covers: shs. 10.00
4. Large duplicate book: shs.   7.00
5. Tying paper: shs. 10.00
6. Carbon paper: shs. <u>2.50</u>
   Total   shs. <u>99.50</u>

No General has any authority to come to the village and ask the people for money or food. He must tell the village KLFA Commander what he wants. Make sure that anything taken away by the guerrillas is recorded for future compensation. Tell our partisans not to offer any money to guerrillas without your authority.

D.K.

Guerrillas to Kīmathi

Kĩrĩma Kĩa Igongona
P.O. Box 29
Nyandarwa
September 12, 1953

To the Leader of G.M. Land Freedom Army,

Many greetings.

I am glad to have this opportunity to inform you that I am still alive. I was delighted when I received your last letter. I was not able to attend the consultative meeting of August 9, 1953, because of reasons beyond my control. Please accept my sincere apologies.

In the meantime, I would like to let you know that the people you sent to brief me about the proceedings of the meeting were not able able to give me a concrete report. Each gave a different version of what he heard and saw. Consequently, I still don't know what we agreed upon at the meeting, and what new line of organization my force should adopt. Please send us the minutes of the meeting immediately.

When are you coming to visit this front? I would like to have a serious discussion with you concerning the reorganization of our fighting forces and the drawing up of a new war strategy. From my own experience, I think there is a need to weed out harmful elements within the guerrilla army. In this connection, there is a great need to draw up a general code of discipline for our guerrilla army to follow. I have found out that there are some individual guerrillas in my own force, who refuse to submit to our discipline, and there are others who don't understand the necessity of carrying out directives to the letter; serious errors are committed as a result.

It is clear that the lack of discipline among our men, the lack of unity in our forces, and the lack of a serious attitude toward the struggle will strengthen the enemy's position and isolate us from our principal supporters—the workers and peasants.

In short, lack of discipline and petty complaints among the guerrillas have dampened my fighting spirit; sometimes I am so disappointed that I can hardly eat. For these reasons, I need your help and advice.

Please acknowledge receipt of this letter. In the meantime, let me know when we can meet. All our troops and their leaders should come up to this side, if possible, so that we can hold a general conference.

Goodbye,
Kĩmbo Mũtukũ

EFI/3/3/601
Wanja wa Gĩtonga
c/o Ihwa
Tetũ Location
Nyeri

November 18, 1953

Dear D. Kĩmathi,

I understand that you want to know why I decided to join the armed struggle. This is exactly what happened: a homeguard traitor called Mũhĩndĩ sent his brother, Karangũi wa Kariũki, to try and persuade me to marry him, but I refused because I didn't know him, I was also not in love with him. After I rejected his marriage proposal, Mũhĩndĩ wrote a letter to my father telling him that we had agreed to marry, which was a lie. When they finally met, my father [frightened and afraid] agreed to receive dowry from Mũhĩndĩ despite my strong objection. He was given 2,000 shillings. I decided to come to the forest in protest. I had resolutely decided not to be married to my enemy, the enemy of my country. I entered the forest on September 25, 1953.

I would like to know whether you approve of my action.

Wanja

Kĩmathi's response was quick and direct; it reads:

Dear Wanja,

...I accept your explanation. Join us, but remember that you are playing a role—a revolutionary role. So do it with determination, commitment and courage. The enemy is a heartless beast; if he captures you, he will torture and murder you. It is a price we have to pay for our national independence. We will get together and talk when I come to visit your camp.

F. Marshal D. Kĩmathi,

I received your letter of December 12, 1953, safely. I agree with you that as a leader's inefficiency is of great harm to the entire force. As a matter of fact, it was this kind of inefficiency that cost comrade Musa his life.

I have already sent one of my best men to reorganize Musa's unit. We have to set up camp at a place called 'Free State', but we have not established good contacts with the peasants; we need your advice on this. Please write to us this weekend.

I have some gifts for you: 15 cigarettes; 10 envelopes; a copy of *Kenya Weekly News;* a copy of *E.A. Standard;* a copy of *Kĩhoto;* a copy of *Jicho;* two copies of *Habari za Dunia;* and two boxes of matches. In the meantime, pass my greetings to Mũngai, Podo, Juma Abdullah and the rest of the fighters.

Tigwo na wega (Best regards).
Gũthera wa Mwĩrĩa

Dear D.K. Matemo,

Greetings as usual.

I am sorry for not having written to you for such a long time. Lately I have been very busy with my revolutionary work.

In an attempt to force our people to surrender, the homeguards, armed with sophisticated weapons, have, nightly, been committing rape, torture and murder. Some of our weaker supporters have consequently been forced to collaborate secretly with our enemy; those who love money and good food have also joined the enemy army and are working against their people's interests. My greatest fear at the moment is that even some of our cadres have started vacillating. One such cadre is Mwangi wa Ngũnga, whose home is not far from here. Since he knows many of our supporters and cadres, he would do irreparable damage to the movement if he were to cross over to the enemy's side. He would have all of us arrested and killed.

I have indirectly raised the subject with him, explaining how important it is to serve our people and country. Since we know how dangerous he would be if he were to surrender, I suggest that you write him a letter praising him for his revolutionary work and promote him to a higher rank for the sake of the struggle. I think your letter will definitely hold him on to our side until we are strong enough to cut him down.

I have sent all the things you had requested except the money orders. I could not buy the money orders because of shortage of funds. As usual, our rule is that we should pay for everything we take from our supporters. Otherwise they will withdraw their support.

There are strong rumors that the British authorities will try to make some political reforms in the country in their effort to weaken and paralyze our struggle. They will announce these new changes by July 15, 1954. Although they would not admit it, the strength of our argument and our fighting efforts has forced them to begin thinking seriously about the political future of this country. However, they should realize that we have sworn under oath, and in the name of our ancestors, that we shall never rest until we drive them out of our country, regain our land and our independence.

What I am saying in short is that you should reject these bogus reforms categorically and firmly demand the total withdrawal of the British forces from our country. You have the support of the majority of our people.

Goodbye.
Colonel Wamũgũnda

May 6, 1954

Dear Marshal,
Greetings as usual.

I no longer maintain personal contacts with "K", but I communicate with him through Reuben, I don't trust him, and I think he may betray me. However, I have tried to persuade him to support the struggle through our indirect contact, but it seems as if he is no longer sure of himself. He vacillates.

In the meantime, I think we should continue working underground in the villages in separate cells instead of all of us working openly. Some of our comrades pose a great danger in the sense that they can betray us if they are arrested and tortured by the enemy.

Thai Thathaiya Ngai Thai
Colonel Wamũgũnda

To D. K.,
This is just to say hello to our comrades. I am fine and well, although I don't know whether I will be alive tomorrow. There is a Gĩkũyũ proverb which says *'mũthigano nĩ ũrĩ nja ndahonaga'*. What I mean is that one of our cadres, Karũga, has secretly sold out to the enemy. I received this information from his son, Wangai. The information is reliable because I don't think Wangai is against his father.

Under these circumstances I am afraid that I may be arrested or killed. In their attempt to force me to give them the secrets of the movement, the enemies may torture me mercilessly. But they will soon realize that I am as hard as steel that I would rather die than turn a traitor.

My advice is that you should try and come to my house as soon as I am arrested and remove any materials which connect me to the movement. But Karũga should not be killed soon after I have been picked up, otherwise the enemy will try to link his death with my arrest. He is certainly very dangerous to our struggle and he should be eliminated as soon as you know about my fate.

If I am not arrested, I'm thinking of going deeper underground for a while in the coming month to try and assess the situation. Comrade Makerũ will take my place.

That is all. Because of the important of this letter, please acknowledge receipt.

Goodbye
Colonel Wamũgũnda

EFI/3/3/103
June 1, 1954

To D. K.,

Many greetings. How are you?

First I must inform you that [Nyĩrĩ] town is under a tight curfew and nobody, not even a woman, can go there without a road pass. So, as you can guess, the situation is very bad. It is now very difficult to get or purchase arms or ammunition in [Nyĩrĩ] town. But don't let this worry you, I will try to get into the town come what may.

At any rate, the piece of cloth you wanted is enclosed. It cost a hundred shillings. I had asked our contacts in [Nyĩrĩ] town to buy it, but they were slow in doing so; so I purchased it myself.

Also, enclosed is the medicine for a toothache which you had requested, plus seven rounds of ammunition. We have not received most of the ammunition and other war materiel from our contacts in [Nyĩrĩ] town; we are still waiting for them, and we will send them as soon as we receive them. Many of our cadres in [Nyīrī] town are doing a wonderful job for the movement.

The last time I was in the town to pick up some ammunition I met a guerrilla fighter from your home area, and was told he was a deputy to General Tanganyika. He frightened me at first because he wore the enemy's uniform.

There is something important I would like to share with you. I hope you won't mind. As the Supreme Commander of the KLFA armed forces and the leader of the movement, you should be very careful and more disciplined in what you do. Every step you take should be well calculated. In fact, you should always suspect those you meet, including your own relatives. I have noticed that you are very liberal when you are among the partisans, especially the women. According to Gīkūyū and Mūmbi customs, we don't disclose our secrets to women, but since the Europeans came women know men's secrets. I would like like you to know that since August of 1952, I have never told my secrets to any woman in order to make her happy.

As I have already observed, you have a tendency to talk a lot when you are in the company of partisan women, and I think this is very dangerous. Of course, it is nice to be in the company of women, but we cannot afford that luxury until we have driven these foreign robbers out of our country. In short, what I am trying to say is that discipline and secrecy are our greatest weapons in this *unequal war*.

Needlessly to say you are the flesh and blood of this struggle; if something happens to you (arrested or killed), this movement will definitely collapse.

We had a meeting with homeguard Mūhoya who ask us to tell you to surrender to the British authorities, so that the war would end. He talked about the humanity of the British, and how they wanted this war to end, but we know that all this talk was a ploy to get you arrested and then killed, in order to weaken our people's determination.

By the way, did you get the letter discussing the Kanyugo affair? How about the money you promised me? When you get some please send it to me. Let me known whether you need a container to put it in.

Please send me the books belonging to William Muturi and Henia—I want to read them. I don't want you to trust the persons whose books I sent you. I am watching them carefully.

Before I conclude this letter, I would like to mention one more thing. The last time I was in [Nyĩrĩ] some compatriots did not want to be associated with me because they were afraid of the enemy. In fact, a few of them ran away when I asked them to help me to carry some war materiel. This really shocked me.

That is all for now.
Nĩ Thayũ wa Ngai witũ
Colonel Wamũgũnda

In response to Colonel Wamũgũnda's criticism, Kĩmathi told him:

...I take your advice seriously; I will do my best to tighten my loose discipline, and to follow, to the letter, KP's rules and regulations...As I told you the last time we met, even if we go trouserless, eat grass and tree barks, we will uphold national patriotism and continue fighting until we drive the British occupiers out of our beloved country. But if we all die before achieving our fundamental goal—our country, our rivers, our mountains, and these valleys and forests, shall testify for our heroism and undying love for our homeland.

Dear D, Kĩmathi,

Greetings.

This is a summary of the situation here in Nairobi:

1. The city of Nairobi is now like Gilgil: there is no corner where a person can hide without being discovered by the enemy. Every African location in Nairobi has been fenced with barbed wire; each location

has one entrance which is guarded twenty-four hours by armed policemen. They search us every time we enter or leave a location. But despite these tough restrictions, we still get through with our *panga* and revolvers.

2. Where the Legislative Council was being reopened on February 16, 1954, it was heavily guarded by armed policemen and soldiers because it had been reported in the *East African Standard* that you would bring 2,000 guerrillas to attack the place.

3. All the Gĩkũyũ, Embu and Mũrũ people [in Nairobi] have been forcibly removed from the Kaloleni and Eastleigh areas, and have been taken to Bahati where they are guarded by the enemy twenty-four hours a day. Both Kaloleni and Eastleigh have been declared out of bounds for the Gĩkũyũ, Embu and Mũrũ. At the same time there is an attempt by the British occupiers to organize the non-Gĩkũyũ, Embu and Mũrũ [nationalities] to fight the Mau Mau. This is worrying greatly; it will be a test of our strength.

4. Many countries of the world are convinced that if Africans in Kenya are not granted self-government and more responsibilities, the struggle will continue unabated.

5. The settlers in the Legislative Council wanted to introduce martial law in Kenya, but they were opposed by six African members.

6. I have already sent the Central Province Committee a proposal that you be awarded the medal of a knight, so that you may have the title of 'Sir', but right now I do not know what the members will decide. If the proposal is adopted, you will be notified in due course. In this case, we will inform the newspaper men that your new title is 'Field Marshal Sir Dedan Kĩmathi, Matemo, KCGE', KCGE means 'Knight Commander of Gĩkũyũ Empire'. The name 'Matemo' is a code name which no one except yourself and those who are authorized to use it are allowed to know about.

I have much to write to you about, but I have many things on my mind at present. Ishmael Kũng'ũ is bringing this letter; he is a trusted comrade, so you need not have any secrets from him. I almost forgot to tell you that your father-in-law is still alive and that I saw him today at 5.40 p.m.

Thai Thathaiya Ngai Thai
Kabũgara wa Kĩrimũ
For the Nairobi War council
February 1954

Editor's note: In response to the letter, Kĩmathi insisted that since Mau Mau was a national movement the new title should be changed to 'Knight Commander of Africa Empire (KCAE).

Dear D. Kĩmathi,

Despite my instructions, Ngire has refused to come and explain his case to you. Yesterday, I insisted that he should come to see you, but after bitter arguments I decided to drop the matter. I have also suggested to him that if he does not want to see you he should write and explain his case, but he has also rejected this proposal.

Under the circumstances, I suggest that you and other members of the Kenya Parliament should visit my camp so that we can discuss this affair together. However, let me know about the day of your arrival beforehand.

With many greetings.
Yours,
General Omera

P.S. if you have any sugar, please send me some. Mine is finished. I have enclosed the daily report of our unit's activities. If it meets your approval, please stamp it and send one copy to me.

Dear Marshal D. Kĩmathi,

Many greetings.

Thanks to *Mwene-Nyaga* for giving me this opportunity to write these few lines to inform you that I am well.

By the way, did you receive the airmail envelopes which were sent to you by Ngarĩ wa Thimba? They were given to General Kimbo to bring them to you. How about Mathenge wa Kĩniũ's letter concerning the sacrifice and the disagreement between you and Mũngai? If you have received that letter, let me know at once.

We have two rams and a ewe which are ready for the sacrifice. We are waiting for you to tell us when it should be performed. We have been preparing people from Mathĩra for the sacrifice up in the bamboo forest.

All the people are well and nothing is wrong.
I am the leader of W.G. No. 1 Icagacirũ

Witness No. 1, from Reserve
Ref. Case: MM/KT vs. Marshal

F.M. Dedan Kĩmathi,

I was very delighted to see you and to hear your voice and that of Commander Ndĩritũ wa Thũita. Knowing how busy you are, we did not really think you would take the time to visit us. Everyone here has been talking about you, and we are praying to *Mwene-Nyaga* to give you courage and strength to drive these foreign robbers from our beloved country.

In the meantime, I have asked the village leaders who work with me whether they had sent you a letter or verbal message about the Kĩbũkũ conspiracy, but they told me they had not done so, and that they knew absolutely nothing about these treacherous plans.

We think that the person who told you about the conspiracy should explain the whole affair to the Kenya Parliament. He should provide you with the following information:

1. The number of persons, besides Kĩbũkũ, who are involved in this conspiracy.
2. The reason why Kĩbũkũ wants to neutralize your leadership.
3. How many other KLFA leaders Kĩbũkũ wants to eliminate.

Since this is a serious matter, we urge the Kenya Parliament to work relentlessly to unearth this conspiracy. The ringleaders of this treacherous group, especially Kĩbũkũ, should be eliminated as a lesson to others.

In conclusion, we want you to know that we support your leadership and we are ready and prepared to defend it.

We send you all our love.
Thayũ wa Ngai Witũ
W.G. No. 1
Icagacirũ Village
March 14, 1954

Central Province
Nairobi Centre

Dear F.M. D.K. Matemo,

Warm greetings from your compatriots, and from our beloved country which today is occupied by Europeans. We will fight to our last drop of blood to liberate it. This land is ours from the beginning—given to us by the Ngai. Those of our people who ignore this fact are as foolish as the Europeans who think that force will crush our determination; but we are going to fight against these robbers until we drive them out of this country. This war is just according to our *Ngai,* and therefore we will fight with vigilance and adversity.

We have received two of the letters you sent to us. We received the first one on February 20, 1954 and the second arrived on February 22nd. We studied them very carefully in order to understand the situation. We are shocked to learn that Kĩbũkũ wa Theuri and his accomplices are planning to get rid of you and take over the leadership of the movement. They should know that only the Mau Mau Central Committee can remove you from your position of leadership, and since you are already doing a good job, you will continue to lead the [revolutionary] struggle. In this regard, we consider Kĩbũkũ and his group as renegades and destructive elements. From *Ngongu to Karĩmature,* we consider them traitors and enemies of our struggle.

Since the line Kĩbũkũ and his group have taken is obviously one of treachery, we have authorized you to deal with them as you see fit, they are no longer members of *Gĩkũyũ na Mũmbi*. They should be exterminated and their bodies thrown to the hyenas

We want to emphasize that we have confidence in your leadership; the Kenyan people depend on you for their victory. Finally, the comrade we have sent with this letter is trustworthy; you can give him any information you want to send back to us.

The war situation is going well on our side, we are sure we will be victorious.

I am,
J. K. Kĩmaigwa
For the African Freedom Army, Headquarters, Nairobi
P.S. Mwangi's mother is still alive and has sent you the enclosed jersey.

M.K. Captain Gateru
Kĩmũrĩ Section A
May 29, 1954.

Dear Marshal D. K.,

Many greetings.

I am sorry that I haven't written to you since I came from Mũrang'a. I hope you don't mind.

I am writing to request a transfer from Kĩmũrĩ Section A to another unit; I find it difficult to work with my superior. Since this is my first request for a transfer from one unit to another, I hope the Kenya Parliament will have no objections. I intend to leave this unit as soon as I hear from you.

This is all for now. Please remember me to all our comrades.

Your compatriot,
M.K. Captain Gateru

June 23, 1954

Dear Marshal,

Greetings.

Wamũyũ is going to Mathĩra en route to [Kĩrĩnyaga]. I got this information yesterday at 2 p.m.

I tried to persuade her not to go until she received permission from the Parliament, but she said she must go because she is expected on July 10, 1954. In this connection, I would like to know whether you would like to prepare a letter to be taken to the [Kĩrĩnyaga] leaders. She is leaving today at 3 p.m. If you are going to write, the letter should reach me before this time.

By the way, will it be alright for me to write to General Kariba (Gĩtĩtĩ) and other comrades there?

Devotedly yours,
Commander Magũ

John Kameme
Nyeri
July 7, 1954

Dear Marshal D. K.,

I have received letters from you twice, but please don't ask me why I didn't reply sooner. Things are tight here.

I am writing this letter on behalf of myself and comrades Karūmaindo and Muturi 5/5. First, we are sad to report that a faithful and dedicated comrade, Kahiū wa Kagoni, was arrested by the enemy the other day. He was of great importance to us and to the struggle in general. He used to supply us with ammunition and guns from Nanyuki. He has the kind of courage that many of our compatriots don't have. Try and see whether force can be used to free him.

We have received a telegram from Nanyuki informing us that war materiel like ammunition and guns are available in plenty there. Our problem is that we don't have the cash to buy these precious things. We also have the problem of transporting these firearms down here now that Comrade Kahiū is in the enemy's hands. What are your suggestions?

In your letter of June 5, 1954, you had asked for sugar. We had some problems getting sugar in this town. I had 4 lbs which I gave to Colonel Wamūgūnda when he was here recently.

Since Mūrĩa Rūnene has not yet brought the ammunition which he promised, we are sending you twelve bullets that we have. When Mūrĩa brings the rest, they will be sent to you immediately.

In conclusion, things are alright with us except that no Africans, except the homeguard traitors, are allowed to enter or leave the town. This is part of the enemy's attempt to isolate us from the peasant masses.

Remember me to the heroes of the struggle. As you can see, I have changed my signature.

Thai Thathaiya Ngai Thai
Yours, Mūrūi John Kameme
J.M.J. Kameme

October 16, 1954

To Sir Field Marshal Kĩmathi

Many greetings.

I would like to inform you that I moved my whole force form Mũtangarũru to Rũthaithi for tactical reasons. In case you want to contact me, I am based at Rũthaithi.

I received information about the last General Conference, but I was not able to attend because I was not feeling well. I will definitely attend the next one. When and where will it take place this time?

How are Mbaria wa Kaniũ, Mathenge wa Mũrũgĩ and the rest of our comrades? Greetings from Nyaga.

Stand firm, the whole struggle depends on your strong leadership.

Yours,
General Kahiũ-Itina

Major Gen. Vido
Kĩmũrĩ Section A
July 1954

Dear Sir Marshal,

When I arrived here at about half past twelve, I found that my force had come back from the battlefield where it had done an excellent job. General Kĩmbo and I had jointly organized an attack on the enemy forces in the Kĩnunga area. The two forces fought heroically, destroying the enemy's post, shops and other property. Several members of the enemy were wiped out. In addition, they seized a full bag of sugar, several tins of milk cream, ghee, two big mirrors and quantities of writing material.

Another important piece of news is that the Battle of Kĩringa ended the complete defeat of the enemy. We captured two enemy soldiers. Our losses were light.

The sad news concerns Kanyinya's small unit. Most of his men were captured and the rest were slaughtered when the enemy made a surprise attack on their camp. The enemy is still occupying Kanyinya's *mbuci*. Thousands of enemy troops have also gone to Kĩandongoro. Consequently, there is a [fierce] battle going on there between our forces and those of the enemy.

Nĩ Thayũ wa Ngai
Major General Vido

October 27, 1954

Dear Field Marshal Kĩmathi,

Thanks to *Mwene-Nyaga* for giving me this opportunity to inform you that I arrived safely and well. Started working for the people with dedication, but we have had many problems. For instance, we have spent nine days without food or fire. I have also had a quarrel with the leader of the unit regarding the new rank you gave me. In this connection, I would be very glad if you could write to him and explain about my promotion. I would like your letter to reach him before I go to Gilgil on a mission.

I think I should come and consult you personally before I make any major decision. In fact, talking to you personally is better than writing letters.

In the meantime, I have decided to stay on the farm in order to have an opportunity to assess the leadership of the unit.

Many greetings from Mwangi wa Ng'ang'a from L2 Unit. You should remember him; he is the Unit Secretary.

I remain,
M. C. W. Kahũgi

November 13, 1954

D. K. Waciũri,

Greetings as usual.

I am well. Basically, our situation is not bad; we are fearlessly working for the movement. My mission to Nakuru was not successful. I was not able to meet our troops and, under these circumstances, I was forced to come back.

The important thing I learned when I was there is that the enemy is forcing the people to take an anti-Mau Mau oath. This new anti-Mau Mau oath is called 'Ekinni'. The enemy's aim is to break our people's resistance, and hence weaken our struggle.

My suggestion is that we should use all means possible to crush this evil propaganda; otherwise it will destroy all our efforts.

We have collected some money and we will send it to you shortly.

Best regards,
Wanjaũ wa Kĩbiri

Dear Marshal D. K.,

I hereby accuse Mathenge wa Kĩhũni of a criminal act against my unit. I hope you and the War council will take this matter seriously.

At about 6 p.m. yesterday, Mathenge and his men came to my camp and stopped us from carrying on with our duties. He said that you had given him power to do whatever he wanted in the whole of Kenya. He accused us of being ineffective in our revolutionary work. When I insisted that he should move out of my camp, he gave an order to his men and within a few seconds 45 armed guerrillas surrounded me and disarmed me. They treated me as if I were an enemy. To avoid a bloody confrontation, I ordered my men not to interfere.

If I try to explain in detail what really happened, you may think I am exaggerating. In short, Mathenge and his men told us that you had authorized him to discipline us because they were the only active and brave group in this region, and that the rest of us thought of nothing else but food. Before I react, I would like to hear from you as to whether you have given them such powers.

Another thing I would like you to know is that Mathenge and his men are insisting on taking away our guns. They said they would kill us if we refused to hand over all of our guns to them. They also said that in future we would not leave Nyandarwa without their permission.

Meanwhile, we have a considerable number of sick comrades and we would like to know where we can take them for treatment. At the same time, we would like to know whether you would approve of a bloody confrontation between us and General Kariba's men. They took away one of our guns by force.

Please reply to this letter immediately; if possible, try to visit us. We are very much worried about what will happen when Mathenge returns from Rūthaithi. We will definitely not allow them to push us around this time.

Yours,
Major M. Vido

Dear Marshal,

Hello! How are you? I hope you are alright. In brief, did Commander Abdullah inform you that I would like to see you today? The reason I am asking you this is because this morning I tried to see you but I was told that you could not possibly see me until tomorrow. This is fine with me, but what time can I see you tomorrow? It is important that I see you early tomorrow because I will be leaving for Rūthaithi the following day. A lot of work is awaiting me there. I haven't written to the [Kūrīnyaga] forces yet, but I will do so as soon as I reach Rūthaithi.

The principal reason why I want to talk to you confidentially is because I am very much worried about the war situation. We do not seem to be making much progress in the field, while the enemy continues to intensify its offensive. I think if we don't take a firm stand, vacillation, rivalry, opportunism and a misunderstanding of war strategy will weaken our position and demoralize our fighting forces. Let us meet and discuss this in depth.

May *Ngai* guard and guide you all the time and keep your eyes open eternally.

Devotedly yours,
Brigadier General Karari Njama

D. K.,

Many greetings.

We are doing fine down here. The other day we were attacked by enemy forces backed by warplanes, but we were able to chase them out of the area. We killed twelve of the enemy soldiers and seized several of their rifles, plus one machine gun. We lost three of our comrades and two were slightly wounded.

We are short of food. If there is some in the store, please send us. We need things like maize, wheat flour, cabbages, potatoes and beans. In the meantime, I will try to contact the woman leader in this region; I am sure she will do her best to see that we don't die of starvation.

Greetings to other comrades – Macaria wa Kîmemia, Abdullah and the rest.

Yours,
General Ihũũra
Iratĩ Mbuci

Dear Marshal,

How are you?
Here is a gift for you – a song!
How are you Gĩkũyũ na Mũmbi?
We greet you with much pleasure and enthusiasm
For we have won the war
The white man is packing

Fight fight everywhere
You sons of the soil
Let us increase our strength
The British are our enemy
They hate us Africans

Cover yourself with bamboo leaves
So that they may not see you
They are evil and brutal
Beyond Kabage there are
Many mountains and forests
where General Muhimu is the commander
And has ordered his army to fight with vigilance

Chania is a big river
Which we cross with bamboo
Each time we try to cross it
There is always a big argument

Their warplanes came to Nyandarwa
To fight Kĩmathi's forces
Hika Hika Ndungu wa Gĩcerũ shot most of them

After the planes had gone
Marshal called a meeting
He said to us
We shall fight them and win this war
Despite their sophisticated weaponry'

What makes me sad and angry
Is the ignorance of the homeguards and the chiefs
Who have denounced this glorious struggle
Who said they didn't want self-government
They wanted the white man to continue ruling us

You compatriot who sing this song
You must praise our fighting men
For their courage and patriotism
But try to improve this song
It was composed in the heat of the battle

You should return it to us
When it is a better song
Because it was written with the blood
The blood of many of us
Who have heroically fallen on the battlefields

Marshal, I suggest that you improve this song and then circulate it to the fighting forces. Patriotic songs like this always strengthen the morale of the fighters.

Yours,
Comrade Puda

Homage to Our Immortal Heroes

Wherever death may surprise us, it will be welcome, provided that this, our battle cry, reach some receptive ear, that another hand stretch out to take up weapons and that other men come forward to intone our funeral dirge with the staccato of machine guns and new cries of battle and victory.

Che Guevara

We Mourn for Our Fallen Hero

Editor's note: General Gĩtaũ Matenjagwo, one of the Mũrang'a's Frontline commanders, was killed by the enemy in December of 1953. When the news of his death reached Dedan Kĩmathi, he wrote the following eulogy and circulated it among the KLFA forces.

Dear Compatriots,

I am sure you already know that the enemy has managed to murder our comrade, General Matenjagwo, while he was on his way to Thĩka town for an important mission. By killing him the enemy has robbed us of one of the greatest freedom fighters; however, the enemy should know that Gĩtaũ's death will only heighten our determination to fight until this country is free [and independent]. His courage and dedication will be a lesson for the coming generations.

In avenging him and other compatriots, who have fallen before him, let us intensify the struggle; let us sacrifice our lives. Let us liberate our motherland.

Field Marshal D. K.

In Memory of Comrade Gathitũ wa Waithaka

Comrade Gathitũ wa Waithaka was a first class guerrilla fighters who asserted himself through his fighting skills and courage. For this reason, he deserves the highest honor our struggle can give him.

Comrade Gathitũ's ability to get along with people, and his love and faith in his comrades was part of his personality. In short, his contributions to the development of our country's guerrilla army were second to *none*. His main goal was the liberation of Kenya and the rest of Africa. And it was for this that he sacrificed his own life.

Comrade Gathitũ was from central Kenya; District: Nyĩrĩ; Location: Tetũ; sub-location: Karathũ; village: Gathanjĩ; Clan: Mũithirandũ. He had worked in Egerton College, Njoro, and other places in the province before joining the Kenya Land and Freedom Army.

He was over 5ft. tall, with eyes that shone like those of a leopard. When he left his job in Subukia in order to join the guerrilla army, he passed through Nakuru town, the city of Nairobi, and then continued on foot to Rwathia Location in Mũrang'a. There he joined a guerrilla group.

During his stay in Rwathia he taught other fighter methods of guerrilla warfare. It was through his leadership that a strong and formidable guerrilla army was organized in Rwathia. He was assisted by Mathenge wa Gatheru. Njenga wa Mũniũ and Ndũng'ũ wa Gatheri. The last two comrades are from Kĩambu. Mathenge died heroically in January of 1954, during the Ndaragwa Battle.

I met Brigadier Gathitũ for the first time in Rwathia on June 3, 1953, when I visited the Mũrang'a front. I was pleased with his intelligence, devotion and commitment. On August 19, 1953, during our General conference which took place at Ngũthũrũ, Nyandarwa, I assigned Brigadier Gathitũ with Colonel Kĩbirũ wa Kanoe, the task of documenting all damages which the enemy had inflicted on our people since the beginning of the war. They were to list the number of cattle, sheep and chickens confiscated; the names of the people killed by the British enemy; the names of our supporters; as well as the names of all traitors. I had divided the work into two parts: first they were to complete their assignments in central Kenya and then move on to the Rift Valley. The two men carried out the work efficiently and with a lot of revolutionary vigour. Others whom I had sent to different parts of the country failed to complete their assignments as well as Gathitũ and Kĩbirũ.

Because of his untiring efforts and extraordinary revolutionary zeal, Comrade Gathitũ got his rank of Colonel in September of 1953 after coming back from a mission in Kararia, Mũrang'a. He earned the rank of a Brigadier in December of 1953. These two promotions are clear proof that Comrade Gathitũ was an invincible guerrilla fighter and a patriot who loved his country and Africa.

As the KLFA Defence Secretary, Brigadier Gathitũ was popular among his comrades; his love for people and his unyielding determination in the liberation struggle were his main strengths. Furthermore, as a KLFA Defence Council Secretary, he was a devoted worker who served the Defence Council with vigour and extraordinary loyalty. He never failed to do his assignment because of hunger, cold, rain or petty disagreements.

The untimely death of our Comrade Gathitũ has robbed us of one of our greatest fighters, but because of his unshakeable patriotism, he will be immortalized by our people. He will live forever; his exemplary heroism and devotion will become the index of our people's vigilance against foreign domination.

Let us always remember Comrade Gathitũ in our struggle and daily prayers and may *Mwene-Nyaga* remember Brigadier Gathitũ wa Waithaka forever and ever.

Dedan Kĩmathi
President, Kenya Defence Council
Nyandarwa
February 1954

> Dedan Kimathi was an extraordinary revolutionary leader, a beautiful human being, but he was also an ordinary mortal who made some mistakes during his revolutionary leadership. Try not to deify him; let history judge him.
>
> Interview: General Mbaria, Naivasha, 1976

Part 5
Our History Should not be Distorted

As a former Mau Mau General, I knew Marshal Dedan Kĩmathi well, since we used to meet in the Nyandarwa mountains to discuss the progress of the war. Kĩmathi had great charisma and extraordinary qualities of leadership. He organized and coordinated the entire struggle despite the hardships we faced in the forest. He was fair and democratic in all his [revolutionary] duties.

General Mbaria wa Kaniũ, 1978

Kĩmathi was a great patriot, a great leader. In fact, I cried bitter tears when he was shot and captured; we always think that if he had not been killed [by the British occupiers], he would have stood with us against those who betrayed our struggle.

Wairimũ wa Maina, a Mau Mau Veteran, 1979

Kĩmathi [is] still buried at Kamĩtĩ Prison. But he will forever live in the collective memory of the Kenyan people. Like Waiyaki before him. Like Koitalel before him. Like Me Katilili and Otengo and Nyanjirũ and many patriots before him.

Ngũgĩ wa Thiong'o

We...acknowledge our indebtedness to [Field Marshal Dedan Kĩmathi], a man who led the armed struggle in this country against the British very excellently. And for that, he paid with his dear life. Kĩmathi died but his spirit of independence, the spirit of liberation, remains alive and that is why the people of Kenya are free today.

We respect, we pay homage to Dedan Kĩmathi and we are very sorry to hear that his widow lives outside Nairobi because we would have liked to visit her and pay our respects to the widow of a man who was ready to pay for freedom with his own life.

Nelson Mandela

Notes from Kĩmathi's Diary

On Struggle

What is it to be hungry and continue to fight for justice? If the line I have taken is correct, follow me, but always remember that only radical change can alter the nature of man.

Lincoln bombers attacked Ũthaya and Chinga for the whole day. But they failed to shake the determination of the people. It is about time the British realized that a determined people cannot be defeated.

A large area in Ngũthũrũ, Nyandarwa, has been destroyed by fire started by the enemy. This cowardly act is meant to weaken our position, but we have already made it clear that we shall never surrender.

The white settlers are like a drop in the ocean among the masses of the Kenyan people, and no matter what they do they will never govern this country without our consent. Our primary aim is to dismantle their evil [war] machinery whatever the cost.

What we have to do is to unite and organize ourselves for a long struggle until we drive the [British] from our country.

The [colonial] government has spent 3,250,000 shillings from October 1952 to December 1953 to try to suppress our struggle. We shall never give up without our land and freedom.

December 3, 1953: A people who can hold secret political meetings, organize a revolutionary struggle, and conduct guerrilla warfare are not ignorant.

My grandfather would have definitely hated and opposed this slave system; my father would have bitterly hated it, but tolerated it. But I march with the times, and I have decided to use [revolutionary] violence to crush it.

Everything has a cause, and the cause of everything is a concrete situation.

I am the light of Kenya, and our torch is my life and blood, which I have given in order that our people, our country, may be released from slavery and oppression.

I have chosen Captain Kagĩrĩ wa Ngumo to be the leader of my bodyguards because of his commitment and dedication.

The Chania River was in flood, so we crossed it by the bamboo bridge constructed by comrade Wanjaũ.

Gura – a cold, strong and swift river; it has four waterfalls. I tried to catch fish, but I could not. It was a terrible day.

Coffee mixed with honey is delicious in a cold place like this.

Pledge

On my honor, and before *Ngai* and many witnesses—some of whom are now dead—I stood naked, held soil in my right hand, and bit the chest of a ram seven times. I swore by *Gĩcathi*, and by the names of our ancestors, Gĩkũyũ na Mũmbi, that I would be in the service of my compatriots and country until I die.

Code

Say "Thũmbĩ", reply "Ngo", if you are a member of Gĩkũyũ na Mũmbi.

On War

The world is round, but human beings are not. Better war than peace in poverty and chains.

War comes but seldom, and when it comes, it brings with it good cheer to those who have won the victory.

War is a natural game for nations of the world, and death is a true friend who will never fail you.

He who fights for the best of his country dies for the best, but he inherits the best he fought for.

The war has robbed us of our best compatriots, but we shall never forget them. They are our immortal heroes.

I lay my trust upon *Ngai* of Kĩrĩnyaga; I will make him my shelter during war and peace.

Life comes from *Ngai,* and only *Ngai* receives it at the end. So we should not be afraid of death.

Ngai does not tie a heavy bundle to the one who cannot carry it.

Dreams

At the beginning of November 1953, I dreamt three times. One of the dreams went like this: I was circumcised on December 8, 1953. On the same night I was captured by homeguards, and then I escaped, followed by men, women, and children who came to demand my release. I flew as though I had wings, singing the great songs of our struggle. I rested under the tree in my homestead. When I entered my house, I found two British soldiers, who had savagely killed my wife and children, sitting in the living room, I shot one dead and the other one dropped his gun and surrendered. There was great rejoicing in the whole village. Before I got a chance to address the people, I woke up. What a disappointment!

On Mathenge and his Liquidationist Clique

Let it be known that some of our former generals are backward and that they are individuals who seek fame, not commitment and responsibility. They only see the freedom of their region, not total liberation of Kenya and Africa. They do not know where Mombasa or [Lake Turkana] is, nor do they know the way from the Cape to Cairo. They love chieftainship, but not work. Let us not be misled by primitive people who hide under trees because they are afraid of fighting.

We have tried to convince General Mathenge that the position he has taken is incorrect, but he has refused to be self-critical and to join us. As a result, we have no alternative but to use force in order to bring Mathenge and his followers back to the Kenya Parliament. We can no longer allow them to sabotage our glorious struggle.

Assignments

Between April 21, 1954 and June 5, 1954, I wrote to the following comrades:

1. The Honorable Secretary of State and the Minister for War, General Karari wa Njama. He is from Mahiga Location, Ũthaya Division, Nyĩrĩ.

2. General Commander Mũraya wa Mbuthia, one of the leaders of Mbũrũ Ngebo Army. He is from Kĩru Location, Kangĩma Division, Mũrang'a.

3. Commander Gĩtonga wa Mũthĩ, sub-location leader of Ituma Army Section No.1, which operates in North Tetũ, Nyĩrĩ.

4. I have also toured the KLFA's major bases and dealt with the problems of disunity in the army, food shortages, and political and social strife among the guerrillas. I addressed guerrillas meetings and explained the war situation.

5. We have told the British a thousand and one times that we do not recognize the leadership of the African members of the Legislative Council. The genuine leadership of the African is the Kenya Parliament.

Report From Battlefield
Mũrang'a Front

April 28, 1953: At about 9:00 p.m. our force under General Ihũũra attacked and overran the Rwathia *hũmungati* post, killing ten tribal policemen and five *hũmungati*. The rest of the enemy fled in panic. The post was burned down. Four rifles and ten shotguns were captured. The country celebrated our victory. The following day, I sent Gen. Ihũũra a letter to congratulate him for his heroic leadership.

May 2, 1953: General Kago's force ambushed the enemy patrol of Kenya Regiment in Rwathia. David White, the enemy regional commander and headman William (native traitor) were killed and their weapons captured. The rest of the enemy soldiers and *hūmungati* ran for their lives. No casualties on our side. Our people in Rwathia celebrated our heroic deed. After the defeat of the enemy, the combatants regrouped to discuss the next battle.

June 2, 1953: I received the following report from General Kago: "We attacked the enemy camp of Icici, killing 15 traitors; the rest of them managed to escape into the darkness. We captured the post and set it on fire. We gained six shotguns and 5 rifles, and executed five enemies; no casualties on our side."

June 3, 1953: Our force under General Kago attacked the 4th KAR camp at Nyakīanga. Caught unprepared, the enemy soldiers scattered leaving the camp unguarded. Several enemy soldiers were killed and five were captured. The camp was set alight. The captured soldiers were shot. There were no casualties on our side.

June 7, 1953: An enemy patrol led by Headman Samuel (traitor) of Makamboki in Location 2 was ambushed by a KLFA unit. Instead of fighting, Samuel ordered his men to drop their guns and run. There were no casualties on both sides. We gathered the firearms they left behind.

June 9, 1953: A combined force of KAR and police sent to Location 2 to fight General Kago's force. Kago knew they were on the way. He moved his force to the Kīanderendū shopping centre and waited for them. The enemy, as it was expected, stopped their vehicles at the shopping centre to harass the people. Immediately they came out of their vehicles, Kago ordered his men to open fire. The enemy caught by surprise, could only return the fire as they retreated into their vehicles and took off. Seven KAR soldiers and three police officers were killed. On KLFA side, there were no casualties. We collected 9 rifles and one machine-gun. I admire General Kago, he is a great General.

June 16, 1953: A war report sent by General Ihũũra was brought this morning by our woman village contact. It reads: Marshal, Greetings. Last night we attacked the Chomo homeguard camp. The enemy, unable to resist our heroic attack, abandoned the post and escaped into the darkness. We killed six of them and captured five alive; we executed them after they surrendered their weapons. We set the post and the enemy shops on fire. We captured quantities of weapons and ammunition and carried lots of clothing and food. Two of our men were wounded but not seriously. They will fight another day. We left the Chomo village singing victory songs.

June 18, 1953: There was a gun battle, according to the Mũrang'a report, between the enemy force and the KLFA unit. A KRP officer Davidson was wounded. His men took him with them as they retreated. There were no casualties on our side.

June 23, 1953: The following report was sent by General Kago. It reads: We ambushed the enemy at the Thĩka River. They returned the fire. It was a prolonged engagement which lasted until dark. No side could claim victory. We captured a light machine-gun, a shotgun and a rifle. We killed two KAR soldiers and one *hũmungati*. We lost one man and several were wounded. We took them to our hospital.

June 25, 1953: Kiganjo School was being used as an enemy military base; our force burned it down.

June 27, 1953: General Kago launched an attack on the Mũriranja *hũmungati* camp. He captured the camp and burned it down. Five Tribal policemen and six *hũmungati* were cut down with bullets. The rest of the enemy dropped their weapons and fled. The captives, in whom women were the majority, were freed. Some of them joined our force, the rest went home. The following day, the British forces attacked the village of Mũriranja, killing defenseless women and children, burned homes and savagely destroyed crops in the field. We shall never, ever, forget these barbaric atrocities committed by a foreign regime in our own country.

Notes from Kĩmathi's Diary

The same day, General Kago sent a guerrilla unit of 10 men to eliminated Headmen Moses of Location 13. He managed to escape with his life. His home was burned down and his cows confiscated in the name of our struggle.

June 30, 1953: The Manunga enemy post was overran by General Ihũũra's force; several enemies including headman Thigĩrũ, son of traitor Senior Chief Njiiri. Thigĩrũ was a notorious killer.

June 31, 1953: This report came from Brigadier Njoro wa Kĩragũ. It reads: At about 9:00 a.m. in Kĩru Location, we ambushed and killed two traitors: Assistant District Jerome Kĩhorio and Chief James kĩirũ and eleven of their bodyguards. We celebrated our victory. Our worries are that tonight or tomorrow morning, the colonial regime will dispatch its brutal forces to kill defenseless women and children, burn their homes and destroy crops in the field. They will commit unspeakable acts of brutality, including castration and sexual assaults.

July 13, 1953: Our force led by General Kago stormed the Kĩnyona homeguard post at midnight, killing several homeguards and Tribal policemen and capturing 30 enemy defenders. Our force seized quantities of guns and ammunition. The post and shops were set alight. The captured enemies were put in one of the houses and burned alive. After our force left, the British force, armed to the teeth, were brought to the village to exterminate the people. Senior Chief Njiiri, who was a running dog of the British occupiers in Mũrang'a county, killed more than 20 civilians to avenge for his son who was among those who were burned alive. The same night, General Ihũũra stormed the Kĩgumo enemy post in Rwathia; killing twenty homeguards and seven policemen. Seven shotguns, two rifles and five boxes of ammunition were seized. The post was set alight.

July 20, 1953: The following report was sent by General Kago: Marshal, I want you to know that we ambushed an enemy force while entering the Nyandarwa forest; killing four African soldiers and wounding a white soldier, Stanley Davidson. The rest of the enemy soldiers scattered and fled. We seized two Bren-guns and three automatic rifles. This attack was reported by the EAS; it reads: A Special Police Officer, Stanley Davidson, the 41 year old soldier of fortune, who has sworn to get the Mau Mau leader, Dedan Kimathi, was wounded in an encounter with terrorists on the western [Nyandarwa]. The four African soldiers killed were not mentioned in the paper.

July 21, 1953: I received a report this morning from General Ihūūra stating that his force attacked the Kīmathi enemy post in Rwathia. The post was overran and set on fire. Five home guards were killed and three were captured. The rest of them dropped their guns and ran for their lives. Our force collected all of the weapons left behind by the enemy. Captured enemies were executed.

July 24, 1953: Our force captured the enemy camp at Mīrira in Rwathia yesterday. The enemy defenders abandoned the post and ran. Seven traitors were killed and five others were taken prisoners. Few our men were wounded. We captured seven rifles and 5 shotguns. The post was set on fire.

July 27, 1953: Yesterday, according to the enemy's newspaper, *The East African standard*, there was a gunfight between our force and the enemy force in Gacarageinī, Kangīma. After two hours of the battle, the enemy troops retreated, carrying with them their dead soldiers. We lost three fighters—two men and a woman. We captured two rifles and a Bren-gun.

July 27, 1953:The Kīariī enemy post was attacked by our force. The enemy defenders unable to defend the post escaped into the darkness. We captured five traitors and executed them before we set the post on fire.

August 2, 1953: Our force attacked the Nyakīhūra enemy post. The enemy defenders put up a fierce fight. Unable to burst the post, General Kago ordered his men to withdraw.

August 15, 1953: During the second week of August, our force under General Kago ambushed the enemy patrol, killing a police officer, Semple-Fisher, before it withdrew.

August 20, 1953: The Gacarageinī enemy post was overrun by General

Kago's force after a fierce gun fight battle. Unable to defend the post, the enemy took off, leaving the post defenseless. Several firearms were captured and 10 enemy defenders killed. This was the second time General Kago has attacked and destroyed the post.

August 28, 1953: Our woman courier brought a report this morning from General Kago. The report stated that the enemy shopping centre at Gakūya village was attacked by our force yesterday early in the morning. Though the enemy camp was within a few hundred yards, not one of them dared to come out. Quantities of goods and food were seized and the shops were set on fire.

August 30, 1953: Yesterday, our force attacked the Catholic Mission centre at Kīangonyi which the enemy was using as a military dispensary. Disguised in enemy's uniforms a KLFA unit of twelve men walked in and without any resistance seized the mission, disarmed the security guards and took the civilians hostage. Next, the KLFA unit seized the medical supplies, equipment and weapons. They took the captured security guards with them, they were later executed;the civilians were released.

September 1953: No report from our Mūrang'a frontline commanders.

October 4, 1953: Two traitors and their entire families in the village of Ngatara were eliminated during the night and their homes were set on fire.

October 8, 1953: The following message was sent by General Kago: Marshal, we attacked the Mīriainī enemy post for the second time. The enemy defenders put up a fierce fight, but we managed to storm the post and burned it down. We killed several enemies and captured five of them; I ordered them to be executed. We lost four comrades and two were wounded. We are celebrating our victory.

October 14, 1953: Six days after the Mīriainī battle, a fierce fight broke out between our force, led by Brigadier Njoro wa Kīragū, and the enemy force—a combined force of *hūmungati* and KAR near Gakūrwe village. Our force was outgunned; it retreated with the enemy in hot pursuit. Several of the men were killed, the enemy casualties was minimal. The same day during the night our force attacked the Kĩgumoinĩ enemy camp. Unable to defend the camp, the enemy defenders abandoned the camp, they flew. Our force collected the firearms left behind and then set the post on fire. The 5 captive enemies were executed.

November 13, 1953: Kago wrote:Marshal, we stormed the enemy post of Mũrirandia after a hard fight. The enemy suffered heavy casualties. The rest escaped into the darkness. We seized quantities of ammunition, a Bren-gun, seven rifles and five shotguns. We set the post and the shops ablaze. On our side, three comrades were killed and several wounded. This is the second time we have attacked this post. Our goal is to liberate Mũrang'a before the end of this year, and then march to Nairobi to seize the government. Under your firm, uncompromising, leadership we will defeat the British occupiers and their native supporters.

November 19, 1953: Genera Ihũũra wrote: We ambushed an enemy patrol near the Thĩka River yesterday morning. Caught by surprise, the enemy returned the fire and ran. We killed a white settler, Lyle Shaw, the leader of the settler's terrorist force in Thĩka district. We suffered two casualties.

December 20, 1953: Report from General Matenjagwo: We attacked enemy's shopping centre at Karũri in Location 10 before six O'clock in the morning. We killed three hũmungati and seized their weapons; the rest ran for their lives. We broke into the shops and seized quantities of goods—food, blankets, sewing machines, medicine, etc. We set the shops and post ablaze. After we left, the enemy troops invaded the Karũri village. They killed innocent people—burned down their homes and destroyed crops in the field, and sexually abused women, even female children were not spared. Our anger is deep; we will make them pay for their barbaric atrocities.

December 23, 1953: I received a report from General Kago informing that General Matenjagwo was martyred yesterday on his way to Thĩka town to attend a War council meeting. General Matenjagwo was one of the great generals Mau Mau ever produced. His death will be felt in the armed forces. Matenjagwo will never die; he will live in our hearts and in our history books.

Notes from Kĩmathi's Diary

December 24, 1953: Report from General Ihũũra: On December 23, 1953, at midnight, we attacked the Gĩthĩga enemy post. The enemy defenders abandoned the post and took off. We killed many as they tried to escape and collected their weapons. No casualties on our side. Before we left, we set the post on fire. Now, we are celebrating our victory.

December 25, 1953: Report from General Kago: We ambushed the enemy patrol of the Black Watch near the Kabati shopping centre. We killed two British soldiers: Lord Wavell and the Kandara district commander before the enemy retreated. One of our men was slightly wounded.

Other Major Battles Fought in Mũrang'a:

1. Rwathia Battle, April 29, 1953
2. Karũri Battle, May 1, 1953
3. Kĩandenderũ Battle, May 10, 1953
4. Kĩgumo Battle, July 13, 1953
5. Kisukioni Battle
6. Thĩka Battle
7. Gĩkae Battle, June 12, 1953
8. Ndakainĩ Battle, June 20, 1953

The Nyĩrĩ Front

April 11, 1953: Our force attacked the Kenya Regiment post in the Nyĩrĩ settled area, after a fierce gunfight our force withdrew. No casualties on either side. On the same day our force attacked the Gĩakanja police post. Although the enemy was able to defend the post, our force burned down the shopping centre before it withdrew.

April 14, 1953: General Kariba wrote: We attacked and overran the Morũgũrũ enemy post in Agũthi. *We* killed one tribal policeman and wounded many. The rest of the traitors abandoned the post and ran. We lost two men and one was wounded. After collecting the weapons, which the enemy left behind during the flight; we burned down the post and executed the wounded enemy policemen.

April 25, 1953: A KLFA unit stormed the house of Metoncelli, a white settler and well-known killer of our people in the Karatina area, killing Metoncelli's wife, his son and his daughter and an African collaborator. Mr. Metoncelli was lucky; he was in Nairobi during the raid. Metoncelli's house was burned and several of his cows were seized in the name of our struggle.

April 26, 1953: Our courier brought a report stating that a Roman Catholic school at Ithengũri which the enemy used as a military base was burned down. The white priest and his staff were not harmed. During the day time a fierce battle involving our force and the British force took place in the Karatina area. The enemy retreated after heavy casualties. We lost two men and several others were wounded. We seized a machine-gun and several rifles.

April 27, 1953: Our force, under General Tanganyika, attacked and overran the enemy post of Gĩachamwangi after the enemy abandoned it and ran for their lives. We killed eight *hūmungati* and seized their weapons. We burned down the post before we withdrew. This attack was followed with a fierce battle with the enemy at the Raka Swamp in which the enemy admitted suffering heavy casualties. No casualties on our side.

May 3, 1953: Last night our force attacked and overran the Gatũmbiro enemy post in the Gĩthĩnji sub-location, North Tetũ. The enemy suffered heavy casualties and ten rifles were seized; the post was set ablaze. This attack was reported in the enemy mainstream newspaper, *The East African Standard*. It reads: On the night Sunday, May 3rd, a *gang* of about 200 *terrorists* attacked the Gatũmbiro guard post in the Gĩthĩnji sub-location, North Tetũ. One of the sentries fired his rifle to give the alarm, but too late. The enemy was already inside. The guards had been surprised in their huts and were slashed as they attempted to come out. Eight were slashed to death. One terrorist was killed. The success of the enemy was undoubtedly caused by treachery within.

Kĩmathi's comment: Through our courage and unbendable patriotism, the British will be forced to admit that we are freedom fighters. To continue calling us "terrorists" is an attempt to distort what we stand for—the liberation of our country.

May 5, 1953: Marshal, we want you to know that we ambushed the KAR enemy at Ihurĩrio, Ũthaya. We killed a lance-corporal and four private. The rest scattered and ran. We collected the weapons they dropped as they ran. Two of our men were slightly wounded. **Note**: This attack was reported by *The East African Standard* (EAS). "Disguised in KAR uniforms, the Mau Mau *terrorists*, about 50 strong, ambushed a patrol of the 6th KAR at Ihurĩrio, killing a lance-corporal and four privates. The rest of the soldiers broke and run for their live."

May 7, 1953: We planned to attack the Ũthaya enemy post and General Mathenge was appointed to lead our force, about 400 strong. The attack took place in the night of May 8th. Mathenge's force fought heroically, but it was unable to storm the post. After unsuccessful attempts to capture the post, Mathenge ordered his force to withdraw. Sixteen of our men were killed and 4 others were seriously wounded, they were captured by the enemy. The enemy recaptured the Bren-gun and two rifles. This attack was reported by the enemy's main newspaper, the EAS. "On 8th May a determined night attack was made on the Othaya police station. Shortly after 1:30 a.m. the *gang* attacked in strength. Blowing a bugle as they approached and opening fire with a Bren-gun captured from the 4th KAR in an ambush a month before, they advanced right up to the wire. Sixteen *terrorists* were killed by the defenders' fire before the action broke off. Four others were wounded and captured, and the Bren-gun was recovered."

May 17, 1953: We attacked the Ihũrũrũ police station. Unable to seize the post because of the powerful resistance from the enemy, the KLFA commander ordered his force to withdraw. No casualties on either side.

May 23, 1953: Our force attacked Kĩamariga enemy post and the *hũmungati* post at Sagati the same day. Both attacks were repulsed by the enemy defenders. The enemy lost one man. No casualties on our side.

May 27, 1953: We attacked the *hũmungati* post at Ngũnjiri village, Agũthi. We captured the post and exterminated the defenders. Seized their weapons and burned down the post. We also burned one shop and ransacked other. This attack was reported by the EAS. "On May 27th, a gang of terrorists dressed as askaris attacked the guard post at Ngũnjiri village, Agũthi. They annihilated the defenders, burned down the post and ransacked the shops. One shop was set on fire."

May 28, 1953: I ordered the attack of Ichara Chirũ enemy post in Tetũ Location. On May 29th the post was attacked, the *hũmungati* fought back, but were unable to defend the post, they were defeated. The post was set on fire and several of the defenders were killed, others abandoned the post and ran. We seized 12 shotguns and 5 rifles. One of our men was killed and several were wounded. I have also ordered the destruction of schools and churches in Ichara chirũ, which the British are using as military bases, and the elimination of teachers, priests, pastors and others who are secretly aiding the British occupiers.

June 30, 1953: This month, the British launched two large-scale sweeps to frustrate our revolutionary activities. The first of them, Operation Epsom, began on June 7th. Thousands of the British soldiers were involved, this including the 1st Buffs, the Devons, the KAR, the Kenya Regiment, Lancashire fusiliers, regular police and paramilitary police forces, and were supported by the air force. This brutal operation lasted for a week. The second operation, Operation Flush, began on June 15, lasted for five days. A lot of our people were killed, homes were set on fire and crops in the field were destroyed. The British are using this aggressive, brutal, scorched earth policy to bolster the morale of their forces. But whatever they do, they will not defeat us.

July 1, 1953: Our force operating in the Kĩrĩmakũyũ area was given order to eliminate traitor chief Reuben. He was liquidated on July 1st. Reuben was wanted for many crimes he had committed against our people. Our people are highly delighted for his elimination.

July 7, 1953: Yesterday our force battled a combined force of police and hũmungati near Ngainĩ School, ten miles south of Nyĩrĩ town, for two hours. The enemy fought with courage, but he was defeated. The three police officers were killed and two hũmungati. Inspector T.G. Price, who was the commander of the enemy force was fatally wounded and died in hospital a few hours later. There was no casualty on our side.

July 13, 1953: On the night of July 12, our force attacked and overran the Kĩamariga enemy post in Konyũ Location, killing five *hũmungati* and wounded three. The rest of them escaped into the darkness. Seized several firearms and burned down the post. They broke into the shops and seized quantities of supplies – blankets, medicine and food. Before they left, they set the shops on fire. On the same day, our force operating in the mũhoinĩ area, North Tetũ, drove off more than a hundred cattle to the forest.

July 15, 1953: Yesterday our force attacked and overran the Kĩgumo enemy post, killing 12 *hũmungati* and one tribal policeman. The rest of the defenders abandoned the post and ran. This attacked was reported by the EAS newspaper. "On the morning of July 14th, a well-fortified homeguard post at Kĩgumo was attacked and overran after resisting strongly. For about two hours the home guards repelled the attack until all ammunition was exhausted. Casualties: one tribal policeman and 12 homeguards were killed. Among the enemy killed were three terrorists and an African shopkeeper who had led the gang to the fort." On the same day, Ichũgũ School in Konyũ was set on by our force because the majority of the teaching staff was hũmungati and vicious killers.

July 16, 1953: I received report today that our force under General Kariba clashed with the British force on the forest edge, Nyandarwa. After three hours of fierce fighting, the enemy force retreated, there were no casualties on both sides.

July 19, 1953: To avenge the attack of the Kĩgumo hũmungati post, the African areas of Nyĩrĩ Township were cordoned off, and during the subsequent screening operations many our compatriots were arrested, raped and killed.

July 20, 1953: Two days ago I ordered the liquidation of settler James MacDougal for the crime against our people. On July 21st our force of twelve men invaded MacDougal's house, two miles from Nyĩrĩ town, killing him and seizing a rifle and an automatic pistol as well as his army uniform.

July 24, 1953: Our force attacked the enemy patrol in the Ragati area, Nyīrī. One of the enemies was killed and the rest of them took off. This attack was reported by the EAS. It reads: Two Europeans and ten Africans under a Special Reserve Officer R.L. Gourlay encountered a *gang* on the forest fringe about a mile from the Ragati police post. The terrorist were scattered round a track on the edge of a vegetable garden and, because many of them were wearing police-type hats, the patrol at first mistook them for another police party. When the patrol was about 30 yards from the nearest *terrorist* it was fired upon and one of Tribal policeman was killed. Fire was returned, but it soon became evident that the patrol was in danger of being outflanked. It made a gradual withdrawal under orders to the edge of the forest. Here it stood fast through heavy fire and three charges of the forest. The Mau Mau advanced blowing trumpets and war horns, but was met with steady and resolute fire. The enemy gradually petered out and, at the end of half an hour; the terrorists withdrew into the forest.

Kīmathi's comment: Who are terrorists, the British occupiers or us? Those who kill our people, rape our women, are the terrorists. We are revolutionaries fighting for the national liberation of our country.

August 10, 1953: I received a report this morning that our force attacked and ransacked the Mūitwo trading centre in Tetū Location, killing five *hūmungati* and seizing several firearms and quantities of supplies. The shopping centre was left smoking. This is how the attack was reported in the EAS. Shops at the Mūitwo trading centre in Tetū Location were ransacked by a gang estimated as 200 strong, armed with rifles and at least one Bren-gun. After looting the shops and killing three guards, they made off in the direction of Kīandongoro. Throughout this period in Nyeri settled area, and the Nanyuki district, we suffered heavily from loss of livestock and periodical raids on labour lines.

Kīmathi's comment: We are not a gang of terrorists, we are freedom fighters; we are fighting a foreign enemy who has occupied our country. Live or die we shall never lay down our guns until we liberate our country.

August 12, 1953: Our force operating in the Agũthi area battled a patrol of Tribal police and homeguards yesterday evening. After two hours of gunfight, the enemy withdrew, leaving behind five of their dead men; two of our men were wounded and one was killed.

September 30, 1953: The following report was received this morning from General Kariba: Marshal, we ambushed an enemy military vehicle on the Nyĩrĩ/Karatina road yesterday at 3:00 p.m., killing seven of the enemies. The rest of them abandoned the vehicle and took off. We set the vehicle on fire. We gained seven guns—three shotguns and four rifles. When the enemy reinforcement was brought, we held our ground. The battle continued for two hours before the enemy retreated. Two of our men were killed and several others slightly wounded. We left the battlefield singing victory songs.

Dec 31, 1953: On the night of December 30, five traitors were liquidated in Nyĩrĩ town. These men were secretly serving the British enemy. Any Kenyan who supports the British must be eliminated. We cannot have traitors and betrayers in our midst. This is what the country is saying; this is what the Oath of Unity says.

Other Major Battles Fought in Nyĩrĩ by our Forces:

Kĩrĩmakũyũ Location, September 15, 1953
Kĩandũ on November 18, 1953
Gaikibii in Mũgutu Location, December 16, 1953
Kangai Battle in Iriainĩ location
Kagumo battle in Mũtica Location

The Embu/Kĩrĩnyaga Front

September 6, 1953: I received the following report from Brigadier Benson Njogu: Our force operating in Njũkĩinĩ forest, Kĩrĩnyaga, ambushed and killed two homeguard traitors yesterday morning; the rest of traitors took off. Two rifles were captured by our force.

September 25, 1953: Our force attacked and overran the Kagumo enemy post in the Kĩrũgũaya area last night. Several homeguard traitors were gunned down, the rest of them escaped into the darkness. Ten shotguns and five rifles were seized and the post was torched. This attack of the enemy post was reported by the *East African standard*: "Armed with Bren-guns and rifles, a Mau Mau terrorist force of about 150 strong launched an attack on the Kagumo guard camp at 1:30 a.m., some four miles from [Kĩrũgũaya.] The camp was overrun and several numbers of the guards were killed and the camp was set on fire. District office Nightingale who was in command managed to flee and the 5th KAR soldiers who came to the rescue were forced to make a speedy retreat, leaving behind several of their dead men." The newspaper continues, "During this month of September nine schools, which the British were using as military bases in Embu, were burned down, three of them in the Rũnyenje area. Three captured guards were thrown in the fire alive; another two were executed by the Mau Mau terrorists."

Editor's note: After the Kagumo enemy camp was overrun by the KLFA force, the colonial forces, armed to the teeth, returned to the village the next day. The British commander told his men: "I want you to use your guns—kill as many as you can; the more you kill, burn, loot and destroy is better. It will make me happy. These are not human beings, they are animals; kill them without mercy. Kill them as you would kill a rat of a snake. If you get tired of killing them, use your penises. That is my order. Now do your job!" (Maina wa Kĩnyattĩ, 2010:167).

October 8, 1953: I received a report that our force attacked and overran the Thũmaita enemy post in Gĩcũgũ, killing large numbers of the enemy. This attack was reported by the EAS; and it reads: "Armed with machine-guns and other precision weapons, a gang of terrorists attacked the Thũmaita homeguard post yesterday night. After little resistance the defenders surrendered and handed over their weapons to the terrorists. The post was set on fire and most of the guards were executed."

October 15. 1953: Yesterday afternoon our force operating in the Baricho area, Embu, attacked a Roman Catholic Mission, which the enemy was using as a military base. Four African nuns and a white priest were eliminated for their anti-Mau Mau activities. We have made it very clear that any African or foreigner who betrays the people's cause to the enemy will pay with his or her life.

October 20, 1953: A heavy gunfight involved our force and the enemy force took place on the Thagana Hills yesterday morning. After a two hour battle our force retreated, leaving behind several dead. On the British side, three KAR soldiers were killed.

November 2, 1953: Our force battled the enemy force—a mixed patrol of police and hŭmungati yesterday in Kĩamacũgũ Location. After an hour of gunfight, the enemy retreated. There were no casualties on either side.

November 7, 1953: In the early morning during a heavy rain, according to the report I received this evening, our force made a surprise attack upon the Kathengũri enemy post. After thirty minutes of fierce engagement our fighters broke the enemy defense and seized the post. Most of the enemy defenders were eliminated, including the notorious traitor Chief Fausto. Our force captured a good number of weapons and ammunition. The captured enemies were executed and the post was left smoking. No casualties on the people's side.

Two days later: After our force attacked and overran the Kathengũri enemy post, the British forces armed with heavy weapons attacked the Kathengũri village, cowardly killing hundreds of people, of whom the women and children were the majority. Homes were burned down and crops in the field were savagely destroyed. This act of brutality was an expression of fear and insecurity. The British know very well that their time in our country is over.

The Mĩĩrũ Front

August 26, 1953: Yesterday our fighters operating in Nchoirobora area ambushed an enemy patrol, killing four homeguards—three men and a woman, and 14 others were killed by our force at the battle of the Sacred Lake. The same day the Catholic Mission at Mojwa was attacked by our force because of its anti-Mau Mau activities. A foreign nun was executed; the native traitors fled into the bushes.

September 21, 1953: Settler Beccalini of Timaũ was ambushed and killed by our force. He was a police officer who had killed countless numbers of our people

Colonial government's comments: As the capital of the Central Province, it was now to become, for four years, an armed stronghold and, subject to general direction from Nairobi, the centre for planning and coordinating the efforts of the security forces in the province against Mau Mau. It was the home town of the Mau Mau leader, Dedan Kĩmathi.

The Mau Mau offensive of 1953 had not, in the Nyĩrĩ District, had quite the same degree of intensity or single-mindedness as the battle of the guard posts in Mũrang'a.

The Mau Mau offensive had started with the Lari offensive in Kĩambu District in March and had then switched to Mũrang'a where it reached its highest degree of intensity in the battle of the guard posts, but was also vigorous in Nyĩrĩ [County], while stock raids on the European farming areas of Nyĩrĩ and Nanyuki districts were causing grave concern; by the close of the period, Embu and Mĩĩrũ districts were being drawn into the vortex.

Thoughts

We stand for revolution, for national independence, for the freedom of our country. Fighting for national independence is not a crime; it is a national duty.

We are bound by duty to fight for freedom to win, defend ourselves, and defeat the British occupiers. No one should disrespect us; disrespect our race and country. We will use any means necessary to win the battle of independence.

The British soldiers and their African allies were brought to the Rwathia region after we attacked and overran the Rwathia enemy post. They cowardly murdered women and children, and burned the entire village and destroyed the crops in the field. This act of savagely makes my blood boiling with anger..

Millions of our people are oppressed and exploited. They are faced with dim prospects of nowhere to work, nowhere to live and nothing to eat. They are pariahs in their own country. It is our duty and responsibility to free them from British imperialism. The British can bring thousands of troops, powerful bomber planes, helicopters and powerful weapons, but we will defeat them.

Revolutionary justice ranges from the execution of national traitors and foreigners who work for the British regime to kill our people.

We have made our decision and our choice—we will liberate our homeland or die in trying.

March 15, 1953: I wrote a letter to Mr. Cooke and to Mr. Mathu, members of the Legislative Council, asking them to support the struggle for national independence. None of them responded to my letter.

April 29, 1955: I sent a letter to Adlai Stevenson, the US Secretary of State. In the letter I asked him and his government to support our struggle for national independence, politically and financially, and, if possible, to supply us with weaponry. The US Secretary of State and his government did not reply to my letter. Now I understand that the Americans and British are allies, they are cousins.

Editor note: This communication was reported by Manchester Guardian, U.K. the following day. It reads: Mr. Adlai Stevenson, the U.S. Democratic leader, received a letter from Mau Mau during his two-day stay in Nairobi last week...The letter was sent through the post addressed to Mr. Stevenson "care of J. Ralph Barrow", American Consulate, Nairobi. Mr. Barrow, who is acting Consulate General, said that Mr. Stevenson had read the letter and informed him that it was from Mau Mau, but did not disclose the contents. He understood from Mr. Stevenson that the letter was "a diatribe against British rule".

Promotions

I promoted the following fighters to generals because of their heroism and patriotic leadership:

1. Gĩtaũ Matenjagwo
2. Kago wa Mboko
3. Kahiũ-Itina
4. Kĩbĩra Gatũ
5. Mũraya wa Mbuthia
6. Ndungu wa Gĩcerũ
7. Colonel Mathenge to Brigadier
8. Major Waciira to Colonel

The Kĩrĩnyaga front leaders:
1. Baimũngi
2. Bata Batu
3. Gacuma
4. Warũhiũ Itote
5. Kariba
6. Mwariama
7. Ndaaya
8. Tanganyika

Embu
1. Benson Thuũ
2. Kassam
3. Kubukubu

Population of Nationalities

According to the 1948 census:

Agĩkũyũ   3,000,000
Kipsigiis   159, 691
Taita   56, 912

Editor's note: We are missing a complete list, as it was drafted by Dedan Kĩmathi.

KLFA General from North Tetũ

1. Colonel Wagũra Waciũri
2. Kĩmbo wa Theuri
3. Mũrĩithi wa Mũkinia
4. Ndũng'ũ
5. Ndĩritũ Thũita
6. Roy Agũthi Location

Tetũ has 14 Generals. Thĩgĩngĩ Location has only one. I would also like to know the names of the leaders of these Divisions:

1. Mathĩra;
2. South Tetũ;
3. Ũthaya;
4. Kangĩma.

Eight Sub-Location of North Tetũ with their Headmen and Guerrilla Officers

Location	Headmen	Guerrilla Officers
1. Gakonga	Joshua	Kobi Wanderi
2. Ichagachiru	Gĩtahi	
3. Ihũrũrũ	Kĩmburi	Karindĩ Toka
4. Karaihu	Mbuthia	Mũtombacini
5. Kũrĩti	Gathitũ	Kiguongo

6. Mūthūainī   Gītahi   Kabaka II
7. Thathe   Mūmbūi   Kīngora Mūtūnga
8. Ūnjirū   Maconi   Kabaka I

Names of famous Patriotic Fighters

1. Gakere wa Nyingī
2. Ihagūa wa Maingī
3. Kabūgia wa Thuku
4. Kanyokora wa Thige
5. Karūri wa Gakure*
6. Karūthi wa Kamweri Hinga
7. Kīama wa Maingī
8. Marige wa Kīirū
9. Mathi wa Gakere
10. Mūregū wa Irimū-Itiatī
11. Mūtegi wa Njūri (Kīrūmūkūyū)
12. Mūthūa wa Mūreria
13. Mūtūngi wa Karige
14. Ndūng'ū wa Kibi
15. Ngambi wa Mūrathimi
16. Ngararū wa Ndūng'ū
17. Theuri wa Maingī
18. Theuri wa Wanjūki
19. Wahome wa Gakūmbī
20. Wang'ombe wa Ihūra*
21. Waruta wa Karūthi

And many others

*Karūri wa Gakure and Wang'ombe wa Ihūra were puppies of the colonial state; they were not patriotic fighters.

Names of Famous National Seers

1. Cege wa Kĩbirũ aka Mũgo wa Kĩbirũ)
2. Gĩcohi wa Ngai
3. Mangũrũta
4. Mĩũra wa Thururu
5. Ngũni

Famous Hunters and Beekeepers

1. Gĩcũrũ
2. Kĩmarũ Mũciiri
3. Mũrage Conjo
4. Njioro
5. Nyanderi

Kenya Parliament
Income and Expenditure Record 1953

Income	Expenditure	Balance
Shs. 47,662.51	Shs. 42,906.39	Shs. 4,756.71

The following income and expenditure account was sent by Commander Ndĩritũ, one of the KLFA unit leaders, to the Kenya Parliament for auditing:

1953

Month	Income	Expenditure	Balance
February	Shs. 4,096.71	Shs. 3,293.00	Shs. 802.71
May	Shs. 20,460.46	Shs. 20,149.85	Shs. 10.61
August	Shs. 6,665.06	Shs. 6,452.00	Shs. 213.06
October	Shs. 275.56	Shs. 197.00	Shs. 78.56
November	Shs. 658.00	Shs. 580.00	Shs. 78.56
Total	**Shs. 32,155.79**	**Shs. 30,671.85**	**Shs. 1,483.50**

1954

Kenya Parliament Income and expenditure record:

Income	Expenditure	Balance
Shs. 6,637.66	Shs. 6,313.92	Shs. 323.72

Money contributed by the peasants to the movement from May 1954 to November 1954:

May	Shs	1,388.60
June	Shs.	155.80
July	Shs.	2,410.56
August	Shs.	200.00
September		Shs. 500.00
October		Shs. 600.00
November		Shs. <u>45.00</u>
Total		Shs. <u>5299.96</u>

Money Distributed to the KLFA Leaders

On April 22, 1954, the Kenya Parliament distributed the following amount of money to the leaders of the army and the Chania guerrillas' hospital:

1. Chania Hospital: Shs. 40.00
2. Colonel Rũanjane: Shs. 30.00
3. Colonel Wangũra: Shs. 30.00
4. Commander Abdullah: Shs. 30.00
5. Commander N. Thũita: Shs. 20.00
6. Commander Nyaga: Shs. 20.00
7. General Roy: Shs. 30.00
8. Karari wa Njama: Shs. 100.00
9. Major Ndũrũri: Shs. <u>20.00</u>

Total: Shs. <u>320.00</u>

PART 6
We Were Betrayed

Time for Reflection

The interviews published here were conducted in Nyĩrĩ, Mũrang'a, Nairobi city and Nakuru district between July and September of 1978. Most of the people I talked to, former KLFA guerrillas, workers and peasants (about 50 persons) praised Dedan Kĩmathi as a great patriotic leader. They were also proud that they had participated in the armed struggle against the British imperialist occupiers and their Kenyan allies. At the same time, however, they admitted that they were bitter and astringent because they had received nothing but humiliation and insults after independence, despite their great sacrifice during the Mau Mau war. They accused Kenyatta and KANU of having betrayed them. They were also consistent in their rejection of Kenyatta's call to them to "forgive and forget". Most of them strongly felt that those Kenyans, who had fought against Mau Mau, raped and killed women and female children, tortured Mau Mau members, burned homes and destroyed cultural materials, should have been mercilessly punished.

Because they feared they might be victimized, the people I interviewed requested that their names should not be disclosed. I will therefore use initials in the following transcripts.

Person Interviewed: GWK

He was a freedom fighter with the rank of brigadier.

Social Status:

A worker.
Q: Why did you join the Mau Mau guerrilla army?

Brigadier GWK:

To fight for our country's independence.
Q: *When did you go to the forest; and to which KLFA unit did you belong?*

Brigadier GWK:

I went to the forest in May 1953. I belonged to General Kago's battalion.
Q: *Did you know Kĩmathi personally and, if so, how would you characterize him as a leader?*

Brigadier GWK:

Yes, I knew Field Marshal Dedan Kĩmathi personally. He was an able and intelligent leader and displayed rare qualities of organization. This is why we accepted him as our undisputed leader and the overall commander of the Mau Mau forces.
Q: *What about the organization of the battles?*

Brigadier GWK:

We used guerrilla tactics to fight the sophisticated British army. Our principal strategy was to conduct 'hit and run' battles, and we were very successful.
Q: *How many battles were you involved in? Did you shoot any enemy warplanes?*

Brigadier GWK:

I was involved in the Ndakainĩ, Kayahwe and Kandara battles. I never personally shot an enemy warplane, but people like General Kago shot several of them.
Q: *How was life in the forest and how did you manage to get food?*

Brigadier GWK:

Generally speaking, life in the forest was very hard and difficult. Rain and cold caused us untold suffering. Food was also difficult to get, and we usually had to do with one meal a day when it was available. Some of our weak comrades surrendered because of hunger.

Q: *How did you get weapons?*

Brigadier GWK:

We seized them from the enemy. We also made our own guns. Each KLFA unit had its own gun factory.

Q: *What role do you think the peasant women played in the struggle for national independence?*

Brigadier GWK:

A very crucial one; since they were consciously aware that we were fighting for the liberation of our homeland, they gave us all their support. Most importantly, they supplied us with food and strategic information. They also brought firearms to the forest, and some acted as Mau Mau spies while others joined the guerrilla army in the forest. They formed Mau Mau war committees to coordinate and streamline the activities of the movement in the villages. I would say that the Mau Mau women were the 'mothers' and spirit of the Mau Mau movement; we could have never made it without their support.

Q: *Did china betray the movement after his capture?*

Brigadier GWK:

People say he did.

Q: *You fought for independence and many of your comrades lost their lives and others were maimed for life—are you satisfied with the results?*

Brigadier GWK:

No I am not satisfied; my only dissatisfaction and disappointment is that our own government refused to recognize our contributions to national independence. We, the freedom fighters, as well as the widows left by the guerrillas, who died, expected a reward—land—for the great sacrifice we made in the struggle; but we got nothing but humiliation.

Q: *Why did General Bamüinge order his force to return to the forest after independence?*

Brigadier GWK:

His demands had been totally rejected by the KANU government. He had demanded that the Mau Mau army should be recognize as a national army, and that all the homeguard traitors should be arrested and charged for their anti-Mau Mau activities.

Q: *What do you personally feel about the policy of 'forgive and forget'?*

Brigadier GWK:

I think we should rather forgive but not forget. How can we forget out glorious struggle in which so many of our compatriots died?

Q: *Where do you see the future of this country given the fact that the majority of our people are getting poorer and poorer while a few are getting richer and richer?*

Brigadier GWK:

Well, I would rather not comment about that.

Q: *Why?*

Brigadier GWK:

We don't trust you educated Kenyans. You vacillate too much. Mũrang'a Country July 8, 1978

Person Interviewed: WWG

He was a Mau Mau guerrilla

Social Status:

A farm worker

Q: *Why did you join the Mau Mau guerrilla army?*

WWG:

To fight for our stolen land and freedom. In fact, our aim was to drive the white man out of our country so that we could rule ourselves.

Q: *When did you go to the forest and to which unit did you belong?*

WWG:

I went to the forest in October of 1953 and was placed in the Gĩkũyũ Iregi Army under General Ihuura. We operated from the Nyandarwa mountains.

Q: *What did think of Dedan Kĩmathi as a guerrilla leader? Were you close to him?*

WWG:

Well, I never had the chance of being close to Field Marshal Kĩmathi. He was a big man, you know. We respected and honored him as our overall leader. His organizational skills and capabilities were excellent; he knew his job thoroughly well. In fact, we regarded him as a person with supernatural powers—our messiah sent by *Mwene-Nyaga* to deliver us from the yoke of colonialism and imperialist domination.

Q: *How was life in the forest?*

WWG:

It was hard, difficult and painful, especially in the beginning. We had to adjust to an environment which was harsh, with wild animals and adverse weather conditions. Later on we adjusted well, and made friends with the animals and birds. They joined us to fight the British occupiers.

Q: *How did you get your food?*

WWG:

We used to get food from the people and we also stole cattle from white settlers. But this became increasingly difficult when concentration villages were set up and pressure from our enemy was increased. During the final years of the struggle, those of my comrades who were still in the forest fighting had to rely more on wild game, wild honey, wild fruits and the like for food. They became more self-reliant. It was a difficult life, but since we had made a pledge to our people that we would never leave the forest without land and freedom, we made the best of it.

Q: *How did you get weapons?*

WWG:

Mainly from our enemy. We had our men in every section of the colonial machinery. It was therefore the responsibility of our men to steal guns and ammunition. Besides, we made our own guns. Also, don't forget that each one of us had a *panga* which proved to be an indispensable weapon in this struggle.

Q: *What were your personal contributions in war for land and freedom?*

WWG:

Not much. After only nine months I was captured during a bloody confrontation between my battalion and the British forces. In this encounter, I personally killed three enemy soldiers before I was captured.

Q: *Were you fighting for the liberation of the Gĩkũyũ, Embu and Mĩĩrũ or Kenyans in general?*

WWG:

We fought for Kenya's liberation. As I have already mentioned, we wanted the white man to leave our country. Many Kenyan nationalities did not, of course, join us in the forest, but all the same they supported us. Some helped us with food, firearms, etc.

Q: *Some of the freedom fighters like General Bamũinge decided to go back to the forest after uhuru, why was this?*

WWG:

The fundamental reason is that they were not satisfied with the outcome of their long, revolutionary struggle. They saw no difference between the colonial government and the uhuru government. They were disgusted to discover that the traitors of the movement had been given big posts in the KANU government and large tracts of land. General Bamũinge's demands were that all the [native] traitors should be arrested and charged for the atrocities they had committed against the people, and that the MM army should be recognized as a national army. Our government was not ready to accept these demands.

Q: *Are you personally satisfied with the outcome of this heroic struggle?*

WWG:

Not at all. We thought and expected that the land occupied by European settlers would be distributed freely to us as a reward for our heroic contribution to the liberation of Kenya. But to our dismay, our contributions were neither recognized, nor were we given the land. Instead, we were required by law to buy our own land from the same thieves who had stolen it from us, as if the price of blood we had paid was not enough. As you can see, we are still very poor; if any-thing, our situation has worsened. I lost my entire family, my small piece of land and now, after independence, I have to be contented with being a farm laborer—earning Shs. 120.00 a month! The person who owns this farm was a traitor—a homeguard, a killer of our people. So I am not satisfied at all. To be more frank, I am very bitter.

Q: *What future do you see for this country? You don't have to answer this question, if you don't want to?*

WWG:

The present political system definitely leaves a lot to be desired. As long as we remain poor despite our brave role in the Mau Mau struggle and as long as these very enemies--homeguards, chiefs, white settlers—we fought against continue to harvest the fruits of the independence we fought and died for, we will remain vigilant. *Gũtirĩ yuraga na ndĩkĩe*

Mũrang'a Country
July 8, 1978

Person Interviewed: WWN
She was a Mau Mau member
Social Status:
Ordinary peasant

Q: *How many Mau Mau oaths did you take?*

WWN:

Two: the Oath of Unity and the Mbatūni Oath.

Q: *Did the peasant women understand the aims of the Mau Mau movement?*

WWN:

Yes, the movement was formed to fight for the liberation of our country. Our country was subjected to brutality by the British, and that was the main reason we decided to take arms to fight against the inhumanity and barbarism [of colonialism].

Q: *How did you supply the guerrilla fighters with food and necessities?*

WWN:

Food was the most important item the guerrillas needed, and we were committed to provide it despite the risks involved. First, we had to cook it at night after our forced communal work. You know, we were working from 6 am to 6 pm. When the food was being prepared, we had to position the village KLFA cadres in strategic positions in order to check the approach of the enemy. After the food was cooked, it was packed in bags and given to the Mau Mau village committee leader to take to the forest. Those women—mainly unmarried young women—who were involved in transporting the food to the front had to travel under cover of darkness, accompanied by a detachment of armed peasants. After reaching the strategic point, they would pass the food to another women's group. This process would continue until the food finally reached the front.

We also had to transport ammunition from one village to another until they reached the guerrillas in the forest. We used clever methods: we put them in a *kĩondo* (a Gĩkũyũ traditional basket) and covered them with flour. If we happened to meet the enemy—homeguards—we would pretend we were coming from a maize mill and the homeguards could hardly suspect us; you know, they were dumb and stupid. Actually, we were not afraid of the homeguard traitors and their British masters, we knew that although they were vicious and could make our revolutionary work difficult, we were too clever for them; in addition to that, we were convinced that we would eventually triumph, despite their ruthlessness and brutality. Those gallant women who happened to be killed in this noble mission were regarded as martyrs. In fact, their deaths strengthened and hardened our determination to fight. Besides, we were very much encouraged by the fact that in the struggle for liberation some would sacrifice their lives for our eventual triumph.

Q: *How was coordination ensured in the villages in times of need? I mean how could you contact the guerrilla commander in an emergency?*

WWN:

There was a Mau Mau committee in every village, organized by the leaders of the movement in that ridge in conjunction with the [regional] army commander. It was composed of both women and men. Its main duty was to organize transportation of supplies to the front, to ensure the security of fighters in the ridge by organizing an elaborate system of spying; to contact the guerrillas in the forest for vital information, especially about the movement of the enemy troops; to eliminate colonial spies, informers and [other] traitors in the village; to recruit youths for armed combat.

Q: *How many members of your family died in the struggle for land and freedom; and how do you feel about the homeguard traitors, and other elements who sided with the British occupiers during the struggle?*

WWN:

No member of my family was killed by the homeguards. However, the atrocities and other brutalities these 'thata cia bũrũri' subjected us to will never be forgotten—they beat us, raped our daughters in front of their parents, put bottles in our vaginas, and castrated men—they caused us untold suffering. Besides, they killed tens of hundreds of our compatriots.

Q: *What punishment do you think these traitors should have received after independence?*

WWN:

Some of them should have been hanged outright, and others should have been detained for a long time to pay for their unpatriotic activities.

Q: *Don't you think we should forgive them now?*

WWN:

No, they are murderers and thieves who now thrive on the fruits of our struggle, which should have been bestowed on those who died fighting for the liberation of this country.

Mũrang'a County
July 21, 1978

Person Interviewed: KWK.

He was an active Mau Mau member.

Social Status:

A worker.

Q: *Why do you think the people of Kenya organized Mau Mau?*

KWK:

To dislodge the British imperialists from our country. They had taken our best land and reduced us to slaves.

Q: *Some people in Kenya say that the Mau Mau struggle delayed uhuru. What is your opinion on this?*

KWK:

This is a ridiculous and outrageous contention. I strongly feel that without the Mau Mau war of national independence, no uhuru could have been achieved in Kenya in 1963. The British wanted to make our country 'a white man country', and they were determined to do so. Our armed struggle dismantled this evil plan. Those who say that the Mau Mau delayed *wĩyathi* (independence) are wrong.

Q: *We have now our land and uhuru, are you personally happy about these accomplishments?*

KWK:

I am definitely not happy. The land question has not been solved and that is why the great majority of our people are still poor and landless. We thought that after uhuru, our government would freely distribute the land formerly owned by white settlers to the poor and the landless, but instead it insisted that we would have to buy this land, our land, from the same robbers who had stolen it from us. We really could not understand this policy.

As for uhuru, I think I can say that I can now walk in the streets without fear of police harassment as was the case during the colonial days. However, our present rulers must rule in fairness; justice and democracy must prevail if they expect peace and stability. The silencing and brutal murder of some popular Kenyan leaders cannot be tolerated by our people for long. For instance, the savage killing of J. M. Kariũki eroded our confidence in the present regime. How many more have to die like this, I wonder?

Q: *Are you saying that the Mau Mau movement was betrayed?*

KWK:

Yes, the people who are enjoying the benefits of the Mau Mau war are either those who betrayed the movement outright, or those who did not support it in any way. Some of them are children of the former colonial chiefs; others are those politicians who built their political careers on anti-Mau Mau crusades. Seriously, something should have been done to relieve the suffering of the hundreds of widows and children whose husbands and fathers died fighting for the liberation of this land.

Q: *Do you believe in the concept of 'forgive and forget'?*

KWK:

No! In fact, I don't see how we can be able to erase the atrocities and barbarities committed by homeguard traitors from our minds. It is not human to forgive those who killed your children, your brother, your mother, your wife, your sister.

Q: *What is your last comment?*

KWK:

Well, sometime when I walk in the streets of Nairobi city and see all these foreign companies—Hilton, Intercontinental and many, many others, I always wonder whether we are really free.

Nairobi County
July 23, 1977

Person Interviewed: WWM.
She was a firm member of Mau Mau.
Social Status:
Ordinary peasant.

Q: *Could you please assess the role the women played in the Mau Mau movement?*

WWM:

Yes, the entire success of the Mau Mau struggle depended heavily on the peasant women. They provided food, strategic information, as well as guns and ammunition (which they stole from the enemy soldiers) to the guerrilla fighters. It was also their main duty and responsibility to transport all war supplies to the front.

Q: *Do you think women really knew the aims of the movement?*

WWM:

Obviously we knew that our compatriots were fighting for land freedom. The white man had brought a lot of suffering among our people, and we wanted him to relinquish his rule over our country. As would be expected in any patriotic struggle, there were a few traitors among women, but all in all, the majority of peasant women wholly supported the movement. As a result, many of us were subjected to all kinds of atrocities by the homeguard traitors and their British allies.

Q: *How did supplies (food, medicine, clothing, etc.) reach the guerrillas in the forest?*

WWM:

There was a Mau Mau Committee in every village which coordinated this activity. After the food was prepared, a few trusted women, usually unmarried young women who had taken the Mbatūni Oath, were selected to carry the supplies to a strategic point where other women would be waiting. They would give these items to the new group of women, and then return to their village. The other group would transport these items to another strategic point where they would be relieved by another group, until the items reached the front. It was a risky task, but it was our [patriotic] duty to support the movement.

Q: *Why was there no fear of the enemy in this operation?*

WWM:

Because of our commitment and undying love for our country.

Q: *What actually happened when you were arrested? How were you punished by the colonial authorities?*

WWM:

The most common punishment was to be put in detention, where we were subjected to all sorts of brutalities. For instance, bottles full of hot water were forced into our vaginas and our men were castrated in front of us. Oh, I can't really explain what I saw and experienced. I feel so bitter about it.

Q: *You have mentioned the existence of a Mau Mau village committee. Tell me more about it.*

WWM:

In every ridge or village, a prominent, able, committed and trustworthy woman or man was appointed to be the KLFA representative in the village. She would be authorized to organize a Mau Mau village committee to help her coordinate the activities of the movement in the ridge. In particular, the committee was responsible for supplying guerrillas with food, clothing, medicine, weapons, ammunition and strategic information.

Time for Reflection

Q: *How many members of your family were killed?*

WWM:

None. But I lost my friends and comrades in this war. A lot of innocent people, including children, were also killed, and it makes my blood boil when I remember them; especially when I remember that those who killed them now occupy the highest posts in our government.

Q: *You mean you don't believe in the philosophy of 'forgive and forget'?*

WWM:

Yes, we have been told to 'forgive and forget', but it is really difficult to forget the atrocities these traitors subjected us to during the war. How can we forgive those who tortured and killed us; those who sold us out to the British imperialists? No, I will never forgive or forget! However, we have a nation to build, and it would be unwise to allow the past to hinder us from a better future. Our last experience should be used to improve the social conditions of many of us.

Q: *Does this mean that you will perceive a future for this country, and if so, under what political and economic system?*

WWM:

Well, certainly not under the present political and economic conditions. I feel that our government must do something to alleviate poverty among the great majority of Kenyans. We expected that the coming of uhuru would improve our lot, but it has been a great disappointment.

Nyĩrĩ County
August 13, 1978

Person Interviewed: NWK.
He was a member of Mau Mau.
Social Status:
Ordinary peasant

Q: *what was the main aim of Mau Mau?*

NWK:

To fight for our stolen land and independence.

Q: *Were you fighting for the liberation of Kenya or for the Gĩkũyũ, Embu, and Mĩĩrũ?*

NWK:

What we had in our minds was a fight to get rid of the British imperialist rule of exploitation and domination. We were not thinking of ourselves; that would have been too narrow and unpatriotic. We fought and died for Kenyan independence.

Q: *Was this war only fought by the people of central Kenya?*

NWK:

No, many others were involved, notably the Kamba and Maasai. In fact, even the people of central Kenya, not everyone participated in this great struggle. They were homeguards who sided with the British against us. The majority of educated people in central Kenya did not even support the movement. We used to call them *taitai (*petty-bourgeoisie*)*.

Q: *Now that we have 'expelled' the Wazungu (Europeans), 'regained our stolen land' and 'acquired our freedom', are you satisfied?*

NWK:

No! First, the *Wazungu* are still here; many of them are still occupying the land they stole from us. Secondly, no land was distributed to the poor nor dispossessed, and the suffering of the masses, after independence, still continues. Thirdly, instead of giving the land back to the poor and its rightful heirs, the land was given to the former homeguards and big politicians. There is no satisfaction in land that is wrongfully stolen twice.

Q: *So the people who are enjoying the fruits of uhuru are former traitors and politicians?*

NWK:

Yes. They are now our new rulers.

Q: *What punishment do you think those former traitors should have received after independence?*

NWK:

They should all have been killed, or detained, or expelled from Kenya.

Q: *Does this mean that you don't believe in the policy of 'forgive and forget'?*

NWK:

Precisely! How are we expected to forgive – let alone forget – such traitors who were responsible for the killing and suffering of so many Kenyans? My son died during the struggle – killed by one of these traitors. I will not forget this as long as I live, nor will I ever forgive the killer.

Q: *Do you think that we could have attained our uhuru without the armed struggle?*

NWK:

No. The argument and strength of Mau Mau dismantled the colonial myth of a white man's country. In fact, the struggle forced the British to relinquish their [oppressive] rule over our country.

Nyĩrĩ County
August 20, 1978

Person Interviewed: MWK.
He was a key homeguard and a vicious killer.
Social Status:
A prosperous peasant farmer. By rural standards, he is very rich.

I approached **MWK** hoping to get his own views on the Mau Mau struggle as a former collaborator and killer of our people. However, he made it quite clear to me that he was not prepared to talk about the subject. He personally felt that this whole affair should be forgotten now that we had become independent. After my insistence, however, he agreed to answer a few of my questions.

Q: *Does it mean that you still think that people still consider you and the others who supported the British during the Mau Mau struggle their enemy, in spite of the fact that Mzee Kenyatta has consistently told us to forgive and forget?*

MWK:

Oh yes. As far as I know, they have not forgotten or forgiven us. That is why I even don't feel secure mixing freely with them, especially in drinking places. This is why I stopped drinking.

Q: *Do you think there were genuine reasons why the people went to the forest?*

MWK:

As I told you from the beginning, I am not prepared to answer anything concerning that subject. After all, why bother about distant events like Mau Mau? We now have uhuru and the white man has sold his land to us, Black people; I think we should be more concerned with national development rather than spending our time discussing politics. Don't you think I have a point there?

Q: *You were supporting the British during the Mau Mau struggle, what was the reason for doing so? Didn't want land and freedom?*

MWK:

I am not prepared to answer that question either, and if you don't mind, I have a lot of work to do.

Q: *What do you think of Dedan Kĩmathi? Wasn't he a great patriot?*

MWK:

No comment.
The traitor walked away.
Nyĩrĩ County
August 24, 1978

Person Interviewed: WK.
He was a KLFA General.
Social status:
A peasant worker.

Q: *When did you join the Mau Mau struggle and why?*

WK:

I joined in 1952 to fight against British oppression, exploitation and tyranny.

Q: *What camp were you operating from?*

WK:

Nyandarwa.

Q: *Did you meet Kĩmathi personally, and if so, how can you characterize him as a leader of the movement?*

WK:

As a Mau Mau General, I knew Marshal Dedan Kĩmathi well, since we used to meet in the Nyandarwa mountains to discuss the progress of the war. Kĩmathi had great charisma and extraordinary qualities of leadership. He organized and coordinated the entire struggle, despite the hardships we faced in the forest, mainly communication problems. He was fair and democratic in all his revolutionary duties.

Q: *How the fighting was organized?*

WK:

First, discipline was a critical factor in our success. Those who proved disloyal, cowardly, bandit-like, or failed in the execution of their duties were tried before the KLFA military tribunal. If they were found guilty, they were severely punished. At the same time, all the guerrillas were required to obey their commander without any hesitation. We also discussed our war strategy collectively before we launched an attack. Because the British army was equipped with sophisticated weapons, we used hit and run tactics to fight it.

Q: *How did you get food in the forest?*

WK:

It was brought to us by peasant women; otherwise we fed on European cattle and sheep.

Q: *Are you saying that the women were the backbone of the movement?*

WK:

Yes, the struggle could not have succeeded without the women who provided us with food, medicine, clothing and strategic information. Some of the war committees, which were the material base for the struggle in the villages, were run by women. Women spied on the activities of homeguard traitors and were also used as bait to induce a homeguard wanted for murder to go a strategic place. Because of their patriotism, many women were subjected to all sorts of atrocities by the enemy.

Q: *How did you get weapons?*

WK:

The main source of our weapons was the enemy himself. We also made our own guns. But we also had our panga which proved to be a very important weapon.

Q: *How did you treat the traitors, spies and informers?*

WK:

Mercilessly! Most of them were hacked to death with a panga. I personally cut off the head of one of the homeguard traitors, cut off his penis, and put it into mouth like a cigar. We had to be ruthless with our enemies to strengthen our position.

Q: *Were you fighting for the liberation of Kenya or Central Province?*

WK:

In organizing our struggle, we had in mind the freedom and good living conditions for all Kenyan Africans.

Q: *You fought hard for the liberation of this country, are you satisfied with the results?*

WK:

I am not prepared to comment on that.

Q: *Why?*

WK:

I am afraid of the consequences. Maybe I will speak on this subject in the future, but not now.

Q: *Why did General Bamũinge decide to return to the forest with his forces after his meeting with KANU government officials?*

WK:

Well, I don't really want to talk about that either. [After I insisted that he should answer this question, he told me.] General Bamũinge disagreed with the government's policy, particularly about the land issue. He also wanted the KANU government to recognize the Mau Mau army as a national army. All his demands were rejected. As a result, he decided to go back to the forest to fight for those demands.

Q: *What about you? Why didn't you follow General Bamũinge back to the forest? Does it mean you supported the government's land policy?*

WK:

This is the same question which I said I will not answer for the time being.

Nakuru Country
September 3, 1978

Person Interviewed: NK.
He was a firm supporter of the movement.

Social Status:
Ordinary peasant

Q: *What was the main cause of the Mau Mau struggle? And was Mau Mau a terrorist organization?*

NK

Mau Mau was organized to fight for our stolen land and for our country's independence. It was a patriotic, anti-imperialist movement.

Q: *Did the Mau Mau struggle delay uhuru?*

NK

No! Without Mau Mau, Kenya would not have attained her uhuru in 1963. The Kaburũ had entrenched themselves and were here to stay. They had taken large tracts of our land, built permanent homes and strong military machinery. Without an armed struggle, they would not have listened to our demands.

Q: *Now that we have the 'land and uhuru', are you happy about these 'achievements'?*

NK

Not at all. My main disappointment is that the people who fought got no land, and their contribution to the fight for independence was not recognized. The land, which we expected to be distributed free to the poor and landless, was grabbed by the former homeguard traitors and the big politicians. I feel that our government should have at least helped the widows and children whose husbands and fathers died in the forest.

Q: *Was the Mau Mau movement betrayed then?*

NK:

Yes. First, those who fought and died for uhuru were not given national recognition. Secondly, most of the beneficiaries from our glorious struggle are the former collaborators, and not the legitimate fighters. Who runs the government body? Isn't it the sons of former colonial chiefs and white settlers?

Q: *Do you agree with the philosophy of 'forgive and forget'?*

NK

How can we forget our glorious struggle? We cannot forget that we fought and died for this land. We cannot forget our history. It is not human to forgive those who killed us, those who opposed our struggle for national independence with blood and fire. In fact, we hoped that these traitors would be punished for their treacherous acts by our government, but instead they were rewarded; they are now our rulers.

Q: *What future do you see for the majority of Kenyans?*

NK

As things stand now, the future for them, for us rather, is grim and unpromising. The political system in our country must be readjusted, since too few have too much, otherwise...

Q: *What do you mean by 'otherwise'?*

NK:

You know, if the situation continues to worsen, our children will be forced to fight—to fight for the same things we fought for. I don't know whether I am making myself clear, but I really get myself disturbed when I see poverty and starvation anywhere in this republic.

Nakuru Country
September 5, 1978

Person Interviewed: GWK.
He was a guerrilla fighter.
Social Status:
A prosperous farmer in the former White Highlands.

Q: *Why did you join the Mau Mau guerrilla army? Where were you in the forest?*

GWK:

I was in Nyandarwa. I joined the guerrilla army to fight for the country's independence.

Q: *Did you know Kĩmathi in person? What do you think of him as a leader?*

GWK:

I did not know him personally; I only knew he was our undisputable leader and the supreme commander of all KLFA forces. He had good organizational skills. In fact, the success of the movement depended on his firm leadership.

Q: *When did you join the guerrillas in the forest?*

GWK:

Early 1954.

Q: *How many battles were you engaged in during your stay in the forest?*

GWK:

Many, but the main one I was involved in was the battle of Ũthaya. Under General Mathenge's command, we attacked the Ũthaya Police station. We fought hard, but we lost the battle.

Q: *How was life in the forest, and how did you get your food?*

GWK:

Life in the forest was very difficult, and hadn't it been for our commitment to the struggle, we would not have persevered. The rain and cold were devastating. Food was another problem. Without the support of the peasants, we would have died of starvation or given up the struggle.

Q: *Do you know what role General China (Warũhiũ wa Itote) played after the capture?*

GWK:

No.

Q: The whole struggle was difficult and bloody, are you really satisfied with its results?

GWK:

To a great extent yes, I am satisfied. There is no more forced labor, no more color bar, and we don't carry *Kipande* anymore. In addition, the white man has no power anymore, we have our own government. About everything else, we have regained our stolen land. These are the things we fought and died for.

Q: Some of your comrades (Gen. Bamüinge and others) decided to go back to the forest after uhuru. Why do you think they made such a serious decision?

GWK:

They were misguided and I don't support them at all.

Q: By the way, how did you get this farm, and what do you think about the majority of freedom fighters who were not as lucky as you were?

GWK:

I bought it; but how and where I got the money is my business. As for the others you talked about, they could have tried to raise money and buy their own land. As our leaders have been consistently telling us, they should not expect free things.

Nakuru County
September 15, 1978

Epilogue

The Mau Mau Anti-Imperialist Oaths

To reinforce their revolutionary commitment, secrecy and discipline, all members of the Mau Mau movement were obliged to take several oaths. There were, however, three principal oaths: 1) the Oath of Unity; 2) the Mbatũni Oath; 3) the Leadership Oath.

Oath administrators were selected by the Mau Mau Central Committee from only those members who were known to be intense in the patriotism and hatred of British imperialism; those who believed in a violent overthrow of foreign regime of exploitation and oppression. In a nutshell, it was a serious crime for any person to administer the Mau Mau oath without being authorized by the Central Committee. Anyone caught doing so was sentenced to death.

The Oath of Unity

This oath was conceived of around 1940 when it was only administered to selected patriots. It became a mass oath in the fifties, and was administered to any Kenyan patriot before he joined the Mau Mau movement. Its main purpose was to rally the Kenyan masses around the Mau Mau underground. In other words, it was used as an instrument for unifying and mobilizing the Kenyan masses against the British imperialist occupiers.

In central Kenya, which was the citadel of the Mau Mau movement, force was used to administer the oath; those who refused to take it were eliminated outright. There was no room for dissenters.

The Oath of Unity went like this:

I speak truth and swear before *Ngai* and before the compatriots present, that:

1. I will fight for the African soil which the European has stolen from us until we get it back. I will never reveal the secrets of this organization or anything concerning it to the colonial authorities or to any other person who is not a member. I will never betray a member of this organization in any way; I will always try to strengthen the unity and leadership of this glorious organization.

2. If I am called upon, at any time of the day or night, by members of this organization, to assist in any work, I will respond without question. I will offer all my strength and energy to further the cause of this organization. I will never fail to help a member of this organization, even if this leads to my death.

3. If I am required to raise funds for this organization, I will do so without hesitation. I shall pay 62/50 shillings and a ram as assessed by this organization as soon as I am able to do so.

4. If I am ordered by my leader to kill anybody who opposes this organization, I will not hesitate to do so. I will always try to trick or manipulate a white man, or any of our enemies, to accompany me; then I will crush him, and take away his guns and any other material he may be carrying. I will make sure that he is dead before I leave him.

5. If guns or ammunition are brought to be hidden in my house, I will take them, and I will never reveal this to the colonialists and their Kenyan supporters. I shall never steal any property belonging to a member of this organization, nor shall I spy on or sell my people to the colonial occupiers.

6. I shall never help the European missionaries and their African converts to ruin our cultures and customs by their Christian activities; I will always support the independent church and school movement. I will never accept the Beecher Report.

II

I solemnly swear before this movement and those of its members who are present, that:

1. I am taking this oath to unite the African people of Kenya in the struggle for freedom and land. I will never sell or dispose of any African land to foreigners, particularly to Europeans or Asians.

2. Should I ever be called out at night, in the darkness or in the rain, by members of this movement, I shall come out without any question. I have committed myself to fighting for my country, and I will never retreat even if blood, suffering and death pour down on me like torrential rain.

3. I shall never inform on any member of this movement, or against any Mau Mau cadres who steals from Europeans; I will never sell this movement either for money or for my life. I will obey without question all the rules and regulations of this movement, and should I ever transgress against them, and I am asked for my life, for doing so, I will never refuse to give it up.

4. I shall always obey any strike called by the leaders of the trade union movement (the East African Trade Union Congress), and will always remember compatriots Cege wa Kĩbacia, Makhan Singh and Fred Kubai. I will strongly support the leadership of KAU and the trade union movement until our country is liberated.

5. If I am ever given firearms to hide by my leader, I shall do so fearlessly. It is my duty to help any member of this movement who is in difficulties or needs my assistance.

III

I swear before this movement, the movement of unity, the unity which is cemented with our blood and the love of our country, that:

1. I shall fiercely fight for the land, the land of Kĩrĩnyaga, the land which was seized by the Europeans. I will never compromise with a European; I will always consider him to be my enemy and the enemy of my country.

2. I shall never prevent any member of my family to be a member of this movement. If any member of my family turns traitor, I will report him to my leaders and have him eliminated. I shall never disobey the leaders of this movement under any circumstances.

3. I shall always oppose intermarriage between Africans and the white community, nor do I ever go with prostitutes. Furthermore, I shall never cause a girl [of our race] to become pregnant and leave her unmarried; I will never marry and then seek a divorce.

4. I shall never drink European-made beer nor smoke European-made cigarettes.

5. It is my duty as a member of the movement to organize our people against Europeans and their local supporters. I am determined to sacrifice my blood and the blood of compatriots for our land freedom.

6. I shall never take orders from European colonialists, nor shall I ever cooperate with the colonial authorities and their Kenyan supporters, even if it means my death.

7. I must recruit all my relatives and friends into this movement, in spite of the risks involved. If one of my relatives refuses to join this movement, I will have him liquidated.

SHOULD I EVER BETRAY ANY OF THE ABOVE PLEDGES:
MAY THIS OATH KILL ME
MAY THIS THENGE KILL ME
MAY THESE SEVEN NDONGU KILL ME
MAY NGAI KILL ME

The Mbatũni Oath

The Mbatũni Oath was taken only by those who were reliable and were renowned for their anti-imperialist militancy and for their ability to observe discipline and secrecy. It was taken by those youths who were being recruited into the Kenya Land and Freedom Army (KLFA). Nobody could join the guerrilla army or elected to a Mau Mau committee without having taken the Mbatũni Oath, which demanded absolute devotion, commitment and sacrifice.

I speak the truth and swear by this Mbatũni Oath, which is the oath of violence, and before the people of Kenya and Africa, that:

1. If I am ordered to burn a European plantation, and to kill the European and his family, I will do it without hesitation. From now on, I regard those who haven't taken the Mau Mau oath, including my own family and relatives, to be the enemies of this movement, and I am determined to fight them mercilessly.

2. If I am ordered to kill enemies of the movement, I will do so, even if they include my own father, mother, wife, sister or brother, daughter or son. When I go out to kill an enemy of the movement, I will take a strangling rope, a panga, a small knife, a pistol, and a piece of cloth to cover my fingerprints, with me. After killing him, I will cut his head off to make sure that he is completely dead, before I leave.

3. If the movement wants my wife/husband for any task concerning the struggle, or to go out on a mission, I will allow him/her to go without any hesitation. I will always obey the orders of my leaders.

4. Should a guerrilla fighter come to me with bloodstained clothing, I must take them away and burn them, and, at the same time, I will provide him with new ones. I will never betray the members of the movement.

5. I will never have any sympathy for any Europeans, be they missionaries or settlers, since they are our main enemies.

6. As a guerrilla fighter, it is my revolutionary duty and responsibility to steal firearms, to protect our people from the British enemy, for the movement. I will do everything to protect the secrets of this movement.

II

I solemnly swear before the movement, and in the name of our ancestors—Gĩkũyũ na Mũmbi, that:

1. If my wife, child, or any other member of my family, becomes the enemy of this movement, I shall assist in his/her liquidation. I shall never commit a crime against my people, nor shall I ever tell lies to my leaders or any other member of this moment.

2. I will never desert the Kenya Land and Freedom Army, nor take a leave without permission of my commanders. I shall never abandon a guerrilla comrade in difficulties without trying to assist him, even if it costs my death.

3. I will always obey the leader of my unit without an argument or complaint, and I will give him any money or materials seized during a battle. I will never hide anything from him.

4. If I am called to accompany guerrilla fighters to a battlefield, I shall obey; I will never give lame excuses. I will never violate the rules and regulations of this movement.

5. I will never expose my gun to those who have not taken the Mbatũni Oath. If by any chance a person who has not taken the Mbatũni Oath seen me with a gun, it will be my responsibility to report this to my unit leader. I will never call a gun and ammunition by its proper name but will always refer to them as Mũtĩ (stick) and Makara (charcoal).

6. I shall never seduce the woman (man) of another man (woman), keep prostitutes, or steal the belongings of a member of this movement; I shall not hate or speak ill of another comrade.

7. I will never take the Moscow Oath, even if I am tortured or killed. If the members of this movement kill me because of my treacherous acts, I shall never curse them with my blood.

8. If members of this movement come to me, by day or night, and ask me to hide them, I shall do so without fear. I shall never spy on my people, but if I am sent to spy on the enemy, I shall never refuse to do so. And if I am ordered to eliminate an enemy of this movement, I will never allow myself to sympathize with the enemy.

9. If I am called at night, during thunder storms and lighting, to fight for our land, to shed my blood for my country, I shall go and never surrender.

10. I shall remain a faithful follower of Dedan Kimathi, respect the KAU leaders, and remember our old commanders—Jesse Kariũki and Dedan Mũgo—until the day we win our independence. I will never serve any government except an all-African government under Mau Mau leadership.

IF I VIOLATE ANY OF THE ABOVE VOWS,
MAY THIS SOIL AND ITS PRODUCTS
BE A CURSE UPON ME AND MY FAMILY

Leadership Oath

This oath was only taken by the top leaders of the movement—the members of the Mau Mau Central Committee, the KLFA generals, the village and district Mau Mau leaders and the leaders of peasant detachment. It was highly secretive. Thus, the top leaders of the movement have to take three oaths

The Leadership Oath went like this:

I solemnly swear before this movement, the movement of armed struggle, a struggle for the land and freedom, that:

1. Today I have committed my life to the liberation of our people, and I will never retreat. I've given myself to be a fighter for my country, a fighter who will never retreat, even if blood runs like water.

2. I will never criticize the leadership of the movement in the present of persons who are not members of the Central committee. I will never plan the injury or death of another comrade. I shall always be loyal to the leadership of the movement, obey its rules and regulations without hesitation.

3. Should I ever be asked, any time, to go and kill an enemy of this movement, I will arm myself and proceed fearlessly to fulfill the orders thus given to me by this movement. I will never abandon the leadership of my people, but I will go wherever my compatriots send me, to do whatever they ask me to do, even if it means my death. I will never run away from the battlefield and leave my comrades fighting. I shall continue fighting until the enemy is defeated.

4. I will work for the liberation of our country until my last drop of blood. I will never surrender or betray my comrades-in-arms to the enemy.

5. I will always work for the unity and strength of this movement. I will see to it that those under my command are disciplined, and that they follow the rules and regulations of the armed movement.

6. I will never collaborate with our enemy, or sell our people and country for money. I will continue fighting for the release of all political prisoners, including the KAU leaders. I will never support the leadership of the African members of the Legislative Council. I consider each of them to be my enemy and the enemy of our country.

7. I will never negotiate with the British for a peaceful settlement until they withdraw their armed forces from our country unconditionally.

8. I shall believe in the movement, in our people, and in their determination until my death, and I shall keep all the vows and commitments I have made here today until death. If I betray any of them, I will accept any punishment which my people decide to give me, even if it is a death penalty.

REQUEST TO READERS

The Mau Mau Reseach Center (MMRC) would be glad to accept any donations for continued research, as well as your opinion of this book, its content and design, and any suggestions or comments you may have for future publications.

Please send all your suggestions monetary donations, or comments to:

Mau Mau Research Center
P.O. Box 746-00200
Nairobi, Kenya
Cell phone 0723-911-371
Email: info.mmrc@gmail.com

www.ingramcontent.com/pod-product-compliance
Lightning Source LLC
Chambersburg PA
CBHW071407300426
44114CB00016B/2217